Waking Up Debt Free

STUDENT LOAN

CONSUMER DEBT

MORTGAGE

PHONE BILL

AUTO loan

TAXES

xulon PRESS

Dedication

This book is dedicated to my wife, Lucia G. Vignola, for inspiring and encouraging me to write this book. She told me to write this book in 1995 when we were sitting at Chucky Cheese on Long Island. "You need to help people manage their money." After she witnessed me working with some clients in October of 2011, she insisted that it was time to write this book. "You need to help everyone with their money now." I decided to heed her words and write this book to help change your life forever. Thank you Lucia for compelling me and standing by me with this book *Waking Up Debt-free*.

I have been married to this marvelous lady for over thirty-one years. She truly is a gift from God. This great woman has changed my life. She has blessed me with three children whom I love and cherish dearly: my daughter Olivia and my sons Rocco and Luciano. Last but never least, she introduced me to the one who has been a blessing in my life, my Lord and Savior Jesus Christ.

Contents

Acknowledgment

I would like to acknowledge some people who have helped encourage me throughout my career. First I would like to thank all of my mentors who have helped me strive for excellence in my career. I want to thank Ray Dublis from The Prudential for telling me and encouraging me that I could break a new quarter record that was set by a TAP agent years ago. His encouragement not only helped me set a new Greater New York (GNY) record with The Prudential for a new (Training Allowance Program) TAP agent for a first quarter break. But, I also set a new GNY record for a second quarter break as well. In addition, I also became the Rookie of the Month and Rookie of the Year. Ray, thank you for your encouragement and belief in me. Then there was Augustine Hong who worked for me and encouraged me to procure the Certified Financial Planner (CFP) designation. Thank you, Augustine, for your encouragement.

Of course there was Walter Wintergerst who hired me at The Prudential, trained me, and showed me the ropes. He constantly pushed me to be the best that I could be. It was Walter who was there for me each and every time I needed help. He taught me how to help people with their financial problems. I am grateful for your encouragement and friendship. I thank you, Walter, for all of your help in showing me how to help people. Bill Furer, a former cohort of mine from the auditing days, has always made me feel that I could accomplish anything and everything and that I was great at what I did. Thank you, Bill, for your encouragement and friendship. For those of you who have touched my life, I thank you also. Thank you, Pastor Mims, for telling me just to write. Also, thank you Jack Wilkerson for taking the time to read the manuscript and for your comments.

I would also like to acknowledge a man who changed my life as a kid, Dr. Dan (Doc) Parrino. Dr. Parrino taught and showed me how enjoyable reading and learning could be and to use the knowledge you have amassed to impact people's lives. The Doc was a caring man who wanted his students to succeed. Thanks Doc!

My lovely bride, Lucia, I thank you for always being there to support me and encourage me. I appreciate you telling me that I needed to share my knowledge and expertise with people who were my clients and those who were not my clients. I thank you for the countless hours you spent reading my manuscript and compelling me to keep going forward. I also want to thank you for encouraging me to keep studying to become an Enrolled Agent. I know your prayers were there to help me pass each and every exam. Your encouragement and love has been priceless to me. Your daily prayers for me to write this book have been felt. There are no words to describe how blessed I am to have you as my bride. Thank you for your love and devotion to me, I love you from deepest part of my heart.

Olivia, Rocco, and Luciano, my precious children, I thank you for saying " you can do this Dad, just do it." I am happy that I will be able to leave you a guide and path to follow.

I would like to thank my father, Thomas, even though he is no longer with me. My father taught me the envelope system when I was a kid. His inspiration in letting me know the value of money and how vital it was to save for a rainy day and save all the time for emergencies. His famous words "you can always spend, but you cannot always save." As a kid, I used coffee cans and painted them different colors to differentiate what I was saving for. My late mother, Olivia, also showed me the importance of saving for a rainy day. She would save money in different envelopes and also hide money in different pocketbooks for emergencies. Each pocketbook she had money in represented a different purpose. Thanks, Mom! I must thank them both for teaching me the value of the dollar and for showing me how to save at an early age.

Last but never least, I need to thank my Lord, the one and only true God, who sent His Son to die on the cross for my transgressions and iniquities and who has forgiven a sinner like me. I now realize why You had me go through all of these hard and difficult times in Tennessee and had me leave the comfort of my life in New York. I needed to feel the pain that others are going through or some will go through so I can let them know that it will be **okay**, if they do the **proper planning,** live within a **budget** and **love and honor you, Lord**. I want to thank you, Lord, for the experiences and knowledge that you have given to me so I can understand the true meaning of money and how to apply its use for You and for every family. You have given me the gift of wanting to help people get out of the financial mess that they are in and to thwart others from entering that zone. Thank You!

I wrote this book from my heart with truth, meaning, and sincerity. My mission is to help everyone to *live a debt-free life*, make the right financial decisions, learn and understand the difference between *wants versus needs* and to be *obedient* and never let *money control* them.

Thank you for granting me the privilege to come into your life and to help you change your life for the better. Remember it's all about your ATTITIDE = 100%.

In His Service,
Rocco Vignola

Prelude

This book was written with you in mind. It is a complete road map to financial freedom. The book contains eighteen chapters that will change your behavior toward money and how to handle money prudently. At the end of every chapter are two pages that are entitled **Action Plan**. These pages are left blank intentionally so you can regurgitate what you have just learned from the chapter and write down what is applicable to your situation. It is important for you to participate and write down what you intend to do immediately. I have noticed when I write down information with my own words and in my own handwriting; it stays with me and creates ownership. Feel free to write down not only what you have learned, but also what action you need to take.

I have written this book based on three factors: (1) I have studied this subject matter in depth and had great mentors; (2) I have taught these principles to others who have become successful; and (3) Last but not least, I have lived through this struggle of money problems through being unemployed. So I know what you are feeling.

This book has no fluff; it is direct and to the point. So everything you read is vital. It's what I call a scoop in a nutshell. Now take this knowledge and commit and adhere to these principles. The time is now to go forward. Go for it and achieve financial freedom and independence.

Action Plan

*A*ction plan sheets are placed at the end of every chapter for you to write down what you have learned and what items you want to address—and in what order. These pages are to be utilized as a summary to what you have learned, written in your own words to encourage understanding. Make a list, in order, of items you will address and put them into action. Check off each item from the action plan list when completed. This will help to guide you as you get your financial house in order and take control of your financial situation. This step is a must to help you move forward.

Watch as you begin to take control of your financial life. Your life will be transformed forever. You and only you can take the initiative to change your life forever. Take it one day at a time. You will see progress and start to feel better about yourself. Yes, it will take time. Time will pass by anyway, so get on board and start to see real change in your life.

The Road to Financial Recovery

———— ⟨⟨⟨⟩ ————

I have decided to write this book to help all individuals who are having a difficult time dealing with money. My passion since 1983 has been to help individuals make more prudent decisions concerning their money and to live within their means. The one common denominator I noticed is that people do not live within a budget. They do not understand want versus need or luxury versus necessity. Just as conglomerates operate within a budget, individuals must do the same. Imagine what would happen to a corporation that operated outside its budget. Yes, disaster! Eventually the corporation would become insolvent and be out of business. The same holds true with individuals; they must have a budget and live within it.

Through my travels over all these years, the majority of people that I started to coach did not have a budget or they did not adhere to the budget they had. They had no idea where their money was going. They did not even know what deductions were coming out of their paycheck. I would ask to see their paycheck stub, and they would tell me to wait and bring me their paycheck stub to view. After viewing it, I would ask a few general questions about their deductions. Unfortunately, they were oblivious to the deductions taken from their paycheck. That's not good! At all times you need to know where **your money** is going. One of the major factors was that in our fast-paced world, they did not take the time to establish a budget. The common excuse was: I do not have the time. Okay, do not make the time, stay in debt, and be broke. Work a lifetime and come up empty. You may not realize it, but the years elapse very quickly. Why make the mistakes, when they can be avoided?

Everyone needs a plan; without a plan there can be no effective action. It's like driving to an unknown destination without a road map. You will get lost and so will your money. This is why I have decided to write this book: to give you a road map so you can reach your destination safely. This book will help you get your financial house in order. You will know what you take in and what you dish out. Also, you will know exactly where your hard-earned money is going. After your financial house is in order, you will need to know how to set yourself up financially so you can protect yourself and your family against the unexpected and foreseen occurrences in life. My motto to all the people that I have coached is, *"I cannot guarantee that you will be rich, but if you follow my advice, I promise you, you will never be poor."*

I embarked upon my career in financial planning in 1983 with The Prudential Insurance Company. I was blessed to have great mentors and an awesome trainer named Walter Wintergerst. Walter transformed my life. A great desire emerged in me to want to help people with their finances. In those days my title was Financial Coordinator, but it did not take long to see I was really a Financial Coach to people. I wanted to serve my clients better, so I went back to school to gain more financial knowledge to serve my clients better and more effectively. I took classes at the National Association of Life Underwriters and earned my LUTCF designation. But that was not enough, so I enrolled in classes with the College for Financial Planning and earned my CFP designation and also earned my RFC designation with the International Association of Registered Financial Consultants. Recently I procured the Enrolled Agent designation—admitted to practice before the Internal Revenue Service. The greatest joy I receive is when I see people prosper from my financial coaching. When people are debt-free and secured with financial instruments that protect them and their families against the perils of life, it's a beautiful thing. It's not only my love, but it's my passion to coach everyone to financial independence. This is the gift my Lord has given me. My life's work is to help as many people as I can find financial freedom and be totally debt-free from the debt that has imprisoned them.

If there was a better way to financial liberty, wouldn't you want to know about it? I will let you in on a secret, ***there is!*** Come join me on this journey to waking up debt-free, and gain financial independence. The time is now for you to move forward and release yourself from the heavy burden of debt.

Psalm 37:21. The wicked borrow and do not repay, but the righteous give generously.

You can tell a lot about a person's character by the way he or she handles money. The wicked person steals under the guise of borrowing. The righteous person gives generously to the needy. The wicked person, therefore, focuses on himself, while the righteous person looks to the welfare of others.

Do not borrow unless you can repay. Almost anyone can borrow through the use of credit, whether it be through the use of a credit card or taking out a loan. The important thing is to only borrow if you can repay. When you borrow and do not pay off your debt, it is like stealing from someone. It is like going to the bank, holding the bank up, and stealing their money. Not only is stealing against the law, but not repaying your debt will destroy your credit.

If you want to borrow money from a bank to buy your new home, what bank will allow you to borrow money from them if you cannot pay it back? I don't know of any. Do you? You will be considered a risk. Banks don't stay in business by investing in or loaning money to people you do not repay. It's too risky for them. Besides, not paying off the debt you created will subvert your credit score.

This is a new age. You need to have a good credit score not only for borrowing money, but also for employment purposes, renting an apartment, leasing office space, acquiring insurance, leasing an automobile, getting an auto loan, and applying for a credit card. Besides, you need to be an example to your family. You do not want to teach bad habits by creating debt and not paying it off. Remember, our family mimics us. Teaching the wrong financial habits will lead your family to financial ruins. Believe it or not, that can go from generation to generation, all because you were careless with your money. Establish and teach good habits to your loved ones.

Understanding
Your Financial Plan

I was coaching a couple on October 31, 2011 in Brooklyn, New York. It just happened to be Halloween. My purpose as always is to uncover needs, to see where the client stands financially, to see what their immediate, short- term, and long term-financial goals are before I make recommendations. In order to achieve this, I use what I call a "fact finder." It shows money coming in, money going out, and assets versus liabilities. The outcome was more of a trick than a treat.

Let's go back to the story. Let's call this couple Mr. and Mrs. White. As I proceeded with my thorough fact finder, Mr. and Mrs. White were asking questions and answering them. When I asked, "Is there any more outstanding debt?," Mr. White said, "No." So I proceeded to ask Mrs. White if there was any more debt. The room was dead silent, with a cold feeling erupting. I told Mrs. White that it was okay to let me know what she was thinking so I would be able to place them in a better and stronger financial position. I will never forget the look on Mr. White's face when Mrs. White blurted out, "I have credit card debt!" The credit card debt was one item to deal with. The taller task was Mr. White. He had no idea about the credit card debt and was losing his cool. Mr. White was trying on his own to get out of debt, but his wife was putting him more in debt.

The reason why I shared this story with you is because to move forward in becoming debt-free, everything has to be disclosed on the table and both parties have to be on the same page. Otherwise, it's like two cars going toward a head-on collision, a total financial disaster. You cannot conceal any financial information from either party. Getting out of debt is a team effort. No secrets! Remember: honesty is the best policy. The truth will set you free.

Proverbs 19:1 states, "Better a poor man whose walk is blameless than a fool whose lips are perverse."

A blameless life is far more valuable than wealth, but most people don't act as if they believe this. Afraid of not getting everything they want, they will pay any price to increase their wealth, cheating on their taxes, stealing from stores or employers, withholding tithes, refusing to give. But when we know and love God, we realize that a lower standard of living-or even poverty is a small price to pay for personal integrity. Do your actions show that you sacrifice your integrity to increase you wealth? What changes do you need in order to get your priorities straight?

People use credit cards because they want what they want and are afraid of not getting it. Buying on credit is not owning the item, anyway. Until the credit card is paid in full, you do not own it. Therefore, don't charge it if you can't pay for it. Use cash! Cash is king! A rhetorical question: why in the world would you use credit to buy an item if you cannot pay for it in cash? The reason is instant gratification. This gratification is temporal. Where does it lead? It leads to financial crippling of oneself. There are many people I know who go out to eat at a Panera and charge it on a credit card. The bill comes at the end of the month, and they pay the minimum or do not pay the total balance. Now the meal that they had at Panera is over and done with, but they are still paying for it. That is *nuts.*

This way of life is not just with food but other items as well. Take a big-ticket item like furniture. People charge the furniture, the bill arrives, the bill is not paid in full, and they end up paying for the furniture even after it wears out. Do you think just maybe the furniture should not have been purchased in the first place? The old man (my father) used to tell me, "Rocco, if you don't have the money to pay in cash for the item, either save up for it, or *fuhgeddaboutit.* You can do without it, because you really cannot afford it."

The problem in today's society is people live on credit and more credit. Stop being so crass, trying to keep up with the Joneses. Who cares! Don't worry about what your neighbor is doing. Be concerned about what you are doing. It's a paradox that in the world's richest nation, millions of people live in poverty. Do you know why? No one wakes up in the morning and says, "Today I want to live in poverty." The answer to the question is this: *"People don't plan to fail. They fail to plan!"*

People need to recondition the way they think, the way that they handle their finances, the way that they handle their daily expenditures, and the way that they understand money and its purpose. This can only be done by a person's attitude. Your attitude is everything and of utmost importance. Attitude is equal to 100 percent. With the right attitude anything is possible.

When it comes to a complete financial plan, you have to examine what it is and know what the components consist of. After knowing and understanding the purpose of the plan, you then have to put the plan into action and monitor it annually. You must understand that the future only belongs to those who prepare for it. Only careful financial security planning can make a difference between a future that is *secure* or a future that's *uncertain.* I don't know about you, but I want the path of least resistance; I want the secure path and a future that is secure. Which situation would you rather be in?

It's okay. You can say it: the future that is secure and certain. Good job!

Building a solid financial plan consists of four basic steps:

1. Protecting your income and saving from the major threats to your financial security
   - Premature death
   - Major property loss and lawsuits
   - Severe injury or illness
2. Creating an emergency fund;
   - Save at least 10% or more of your earnings, until you have amassed 6 to 12 months of your income. (This is extremely vital to your survival)
3. Accumulating money for the future
   - Education
   - Business and Investment Opportunities
   - Major Purchases
   - Retirement
4. Analyzing Your Results
   - Reviewing your financial plan annually to determine if any adjustments have to be made to continue to meet your needs.

A financial plan establishes direction, sets goals, solves problems, and creates money. The total financial plan will involve tax planning, estate planning, insurance planning, investment planning, and retirement planning. The four basis steps to a financial plan and the total financial plan will be discussed chapter by chapter.

But before we can indulge in this, we first must create a budget. I personally adhere to a budget and update it accordingly. I update it so I can stay on track with my financial plan. I also prepare a balance sheet to determine my net worth and update that annually. The balance sheet will show me what I own and what I owe and presents a bird's-eye view of my net worth, so

I can determine if I am growing and if I need to make any adjustments to my budget. A budget helps you plan for the future; whereas an income statement is based on the past. Therefore a budget is needed for you to move forward. If you want to live comfortable and build wealth, you need to have a budget and adhere to it. Just as successful companies work within a budget to keep themselves solvent and are able to thrive with good financial decisions, the same holds true for individuals. A budget is paramount.

Your financial decisions affect others, too. A financial house that is not in order affects your job, marriage, kids, family, friends, relationships, attitude, emotions, physical being, as well as your spiritual walk. Don't let this happen to you or your family. You have heard the cliché that money is the root of all evil. The truth is, the *misuse* of money is the root of all evil.

Action Plan

_____
_____
_____
_____
_____
_____
_____
_____
_____
_____
_____
_____
_____
_____
_____
_____
_____
_____
_____
_____
_____
_____
_____
_____
_____
_____
_____
_____
_____
_____
_____

Action Plan

_____

_____

_____

_____

_____

_____

_____

_____

_____

_____

_____

_____

_____

_____

_____

_____

_____

_____

_____

_____

_____

_____

_____

_____

_____

_____

Your Budget

One of the first questions I ask new clients is, "what's important about money to you?" The conversation usually goes like this: "Today we are getting together to discuss how you can make more intelligent decisions about your money. If this was not true, we would not be getting together today. But in order for me to help you make more intelligent decisions about your money, you need to help me understand *what's important about money to you?* The response I usually receive is, "no one has ever asked me this question before. You have given me something to think about." Yes, I definitely give people something to ponder assiduously. Am I right or wrong? If you cannot make intelligent decisions about your money and understand the principles of money, how will you ever be able you manage your money? How will you live debt free? You can't!

Let's be candid, we toil and labor to earn a living. But what we do with that money is so important. Many people just work with no direction or plan of action. They do, what I call "things perfunctory." That is why I ask the question, "what's important about money to you?" You need to uncover and disclose this to yourself, so you will be able to handle your money and finances prudently. If you do not know what's important about money to you, then how will you be able to construct a budget that is personally meaningful to you. You can't! You need to ponder this question and write down the answers. Apparently, you need to understand the importance of money to you. For example, is it for biological needs, travel, retirement, investing, education, paying off debt, and so forth? Once you understand and identify the importance of money to you, you will be able to construct a budget that is meaningful and has direction to consummate your needs and aspirations.

Back in October 2011, I was in Brooklyn, New York, with one of my clients. This woman has been a professor for over 25 years, earning approximately $100k per year. She does not own a home, has no investments, no savings, no emergency fund, and no money for education for her three children. Her mother gives her money to help defray some of her expenses, even though she nets $75,000 per year—that's $1442 per week. Where is all that money going to? Why is she broke? Why doesn't she have any money saved? Not a dime! The reason why she has no money saved and needs help from her mother is because she doesn't have a budget. She has no idea where her money is going. She spends an enormous amount of money eating out. She buys too many items for her kids that are unimportant: CDs, DVDs, concerts, software, designer clothes and pays for them by using a credit card instead of using cash. Why?

During my needs analysis I uncovered that she was overpaying for auto insurance and renters insurance by 50 percent. Her deductibles needed to be adjusted, and she had no life insurance to replace her income in case of her premature death. Her children would have to rely on Grandma for money. Grandma is no spring chicken and would be left with an enormous burden. After I coached her, together we devised a budget to get her on the right track financially. I introduced her to the envelope system. The envelope system will help you to keep a cap on your monthly expenses. Every time you get paid, you put an allocated amount into the envelope to cover that expense. For example: food, transportation, entertainment, rent, utilities, insurance and so on. Once the bill arrives, you will go into the envelope to pay that bill. If the envelope is empty after you paid that bill, that is it for that month. You are not allowed to spend any more on that item. If there is money left over, I will show you how to make that money multiply. I will discuss the envelope system in detail a little later on.

I cannot overemphasize the importance of a budget. Only through a budget can an individual achieve financial independence and be free from debt. When you are in debt, you become a slave to that institution or individual. My father always taught me to pay for everything in cash. Do not become a slave to any item or object. He also taught me the importance of paying off a mortgage early and becoming totally independent of owing money to anyone. Besides, you will save an enormous amount of money by paying a mortgage off early. I will discuss mortgages later in the book.

Proverbs 22:7. The rich rule over the poor, and the borrower is a servant to the lender.

The borrower must realize that until the loan is repaid, he or she is a servant to the individual or institution that made it. Does this mean we should never borrow? No, but it warns us never to take on a loan without carefully examining our ability to repay it. A loan we can handle is enabling; a loan we can't handle is enslaving. The borrower must realize that until the loan is repaid, he or she is a servant to the individual or institution that made it.

Back in August of 2004, I uprooted my family from New York and moved to Tennessee. The reason for the move is immaterial. But before I did make the move, I made certain I had a position lined up. Unfortunately, the position fell through, and I was confronted with being in a strange land and being unemployed. I went from job to job, but with no success. It is very difficult to seek employment when you are a stranger with no connections. The bills kept arriving each and every month on time. It's a funny thing, bills are never late. They always find their way to your mailbox and into your hands. The problem was I was idled, unemployed with no secure prospects at my disposal. I worked odd jobs whenever someone gave me a chance to work. I was grateful for each and every job even though the jobs never paid enough to meet my expenses.

You are probably saying to yourself how could this guy with all this experience be underemployed or unemployed. My age was one factor, and due to the economy, no one wanted to pay me any serious money for my talent. The majority of time positions were offered to me, they were commission-based. I had to drive 150 to 200 miles a day to see prospects who may not even be home. You can do the math; I spent a lot of money for gas. It was a very difficult time for me and my family. I was in uncharted waters. In New York, I was used to taking control and just doing it. Yes, in New York I was blessed to have been very well compensated. But this is was not New York, and these were different times. I was unable to meet my monthly obligations with just my current income. In addition, throughout those nine years, I was unemployed a lot. When I was blessed to be employed, I was way underemployed. My three children attended college during those eight years. Some years, just one child was in college; some years, two children were in college. By my daughter's last semester, I had three children in college all at once. Talk about financial juggling.

With my situation, I should have been out on the street within six months of moving to Tennessee. The only reason why I did not lose everything was because I lived within a budget in New York and also in Tennessee. I am thankful that I was given good guidance with money matters from my father. But in 1983 when I joined The Prudential, as I previously mentioned, I had very good mentors. I quickly learned the importance of budgeting, which in those days I referred to it as cash management. I instilled in my household to live on a budget, save for a rainy day (emergency fund), and invest at a young age and do it consistently. Yes, there were times I wanted to spend extravagantly and buy expensive cars. But for what, what was it going to prove? My father taught me that you can always spend money, but you cannot always save it. I am not by any means telling you to be parsimonious and divest yourself of necessities. But did I really have to buy a Mercedes Benz or a BMW, or do you have to buy one? We have to think prudently with our money. After all, *only two things earn money; people earn money and money earns money.*

Since I have adhered to these principles for decades and always lived within a budget, I was able to sustain my family and myself when we moved to Tennessee even though I was underemployed or unemployed. My children's education was paid for because I started to invest and save for them when they were 15 days old. There was nothing magical or special about me. It was just my attitude of being prepared for the future. Being prepared for those unexpected events that life hits you with. I do thank God that He gave me the will and knowledge to be prepared for the calamities of life. You can place yourself and your family in a financially secure position also. But you must heed to what I tell you. You must *listen* and be *teachable.* If you decide to do those two things, listen and be teachable, I will show you how to keep yourself and your family secure always. It all starts with a *budget.* By the way, I always used the envelope system my father taught me decades ago. It works!

I still use the envelope system today. It is also what I learned when I took financial planning classes decades ago. You can modify and condense it, but I personally go the extra step and stay detailed. Some people may think and say I am redundant. I am not redundant; I am thorough. The more detailed the better. You want to have a bird's-eye view of where your finances are. Once you become adept at budgeting, you can consolidate. But for now, let's go the extra mile. It will pay off.

For a 30-day period I want you to record all of your expenditures. Use a little tablet that you can carry with you daily. Don't forget the pen. Record every single item you spend your money on, even if you spend five cents on an item. No, I am not being petty. I want you to see how the little expenditures add up and become big expenses that you do not realize. The little expenses that we don't account for that are a waste of our earned money. You will be amazed at how much you are spending after 30 days and never realized it. Numbers don't lie. You will be accountable for your money. Don't try to cheat, because you are being watched. You will learn a lot about how your money is being spent.

The Envelope System:
I have a separate envelope for each of my expenses:

- mortgage payment or rent payment
- real estate taxes
- telephone—land line
- telephone—cell
- gas
- electric
- credit cards—have an envelope for each credit card
- insurance—auto
- insurance—life
- insurance—major medical / dental
- personal loans
- student loans
- other debts—envelope for each one
- food
- education expense
- clothing

- entertainment
- gasoline
- tithe
- savings
- pocket money
- investments—have an envelope for each investment

** Federal Income Taxes—if self employed
** State Income Taxes—if self employed
** Local Income Taxes—if self employed
** FICA Taxes—if self employed

** Envelopes are used for these items if you are self-employed. If you receive a W-2 from your employer you can discard these items.

Have an envelope for any other expense or savings item you have.

Wow, what a lot of work to do! Soooo many envelopes. Yes, you are right! Yes, you can consolidate if you are adept at budgeting and have been fruitful at it. But for now, the more detailed your system, the better. As you deposit money into each of these envelopes every time you get paid, you will feel the pain of seeing where your hard-earned money is going. " No pain, no gain" is the saying. As you deposit this money into these envelopes, your stomach will turn and you will wonder if there is a better way? Yes, there is a better way, but we are not there yet. Let's take one thing at a time. As you are withdrawing your money from these envelopes and paying your bills, you should be saying, "Wow, I am spending a lot of money on that item. Do I really need it? Can I get that expense more under control?" What I want you to realize is that you can tighten your belt just as I did and am still doing. Do I really need all of those channels from the cable company when I do not have the time to view them? Do I need to drive that gas guzzler or expensive car that I have a note on? Of course you do not. Then why are you doing that? The auto industry and the cable company love you. You do not need all those bells and whistles. Remember, it's all about attitude. **Attitude = 100 percent.** Attitude is a frame of mind, and your mind has to be in the right place and thinking correctly.

A   T   T   I   T   U   D   E
(1+20+20+9+20+21+4+5) = 100%

Just to let you know, it was difficult for me to make an attitude adjustment. But I refused to pay for things that I did not need and for things I had no time for. Why make companies rich when you can build your financial wealth? Before I make a purchase, I think of its useful life, why I think I need it. What purpose will it serve? What is the cost factor? Can I do without it? Don't misconstrue what I am saying. If your washing machine broke down and you had it for many years, you need to decide, do I repair it or replace it? I am not suggesting that you do without a washing machine. What I am suggesting is, does it makes financial sense to buy a new one? If it does, do you need all the bells and whistles? Once again, it becomes needs versus wants. You must put everything in a proper prospective. It is all an *attitude*. Once your *attitude* changes, your way of thinking will change. Then your financial picture will change because you have taken the first step to financial freedom, financial independence; you are ready to create a budget that you can live by and adhere to.

A budget is a simple plan for how to spend your money and have control over it. It allows you to plan ahead. You will list various sources of income:

- Salary
- Interest

- Dividends
- Rents
- Notes
- Income tax refund
- Other

Then make a list of all the monthly expenditures in your home.

Fixed Expenses:
- Tithe
- Mortgage Payment(s)
- Property Taxes
- Insurance (Home)
- Automobile Note
- Federal Income Taxes (if taxes are deducted, ignore)
- State Income Taxes (if taxes are deducted, ignore)
- City Income Taxes (if taxes are deducted, ignore)
- FICA (social security taxes) (if taxes are deducted, ignore)

Variable Expenses:
- Food
- Outstanding Debts
- Utilities
- Entertainment
- Medical/Dental
- Clothing / Personal Care
- Insurance (Life, Health, Auto)
- Savings
- Pocket Money
- Miscellaneous

The above is a typical example of items that are listed in a budget. There are many individuals who recommend this type of a budget format. I use a different format and have coached thousands upon thousands of individuals to use the following format. I have also trained scores of trainers to use the same format that I use. You use whatever you feel most comfortable with. Remember the key is to get started. The budget format I utilize is in conjunction with my envelope system. You can use a spreadsheet, a white or yellow sheet of paper, or make a copy of the one in the book—whatever you prefer.

Your Total Salary _____

Spouse's Total Salary _____

Total Income _____

Monthly Expenditures:

Home Mortgage/Rent _____

Real Estates Taxes _____

Telephone/Cable _____

Gas/Utilities _____

Fuel-Oil _____

Credit Cards _____

Insurance (Auto/Home) _____

Insurance (Life/Health) _____

Medical Bills _____

Loans/Debts _____

Transportation	_____
Food/Groceries	_____
Education	_____
Clothing	_____
Entertainment	_____
Gasoline	_____
Payroll Taxes	_____
Pocket Money	_____
Savings	_____
Tithe	_____
Other	_____
Other	_____
Total Expenses	_____
Net Surplus/Deficit	_____

Example on how to utilize this form.

I always look at the paystub the see all of the deductions that are listed. I work with net income so I know exactly what the individual is bringing home. It's not how much you earn, it's how much you have left over after your expenses. That's why you have to control your expenses and save.

All expenses have to be reviewed over a 12-month period. Add the total of each item over 12 months, take that total and divide by 12 to yield your monthly expense. Then list each item on the budget form. Example: Tony works as an accountant, earning $105,600 per year. His wife, Maria, is a housewife looking to be a writer. At present, there are no children. Tony pays $20,000 per year in payroll taxes. His monthly expenses are as follows: Mortgage $700, Real Estate Taxes $150, Telephone $180,Cable $150, Gas $30, Electric $90, Water $180, Credit Cards $75, Auto Insurance $210, Life Insurance $330, Homeowner's Insurance $50, Medical Insurance $285, Doctor Bills $15, Food/Groceries $2,000, Tithe $880, Clothing $100, Entertainment $80, Gasoline $300, Savings $900, Pocket Money for Tony $200, Pocket money for Maria $100.

Your Total Salary (Tony)	8,800
Spouse's Total Salary (Maria)	0
Total Income	8,800

Monthly Expenditures:

Home Mortgage/Rent	700
Real Estates Taxes	150
Telephone/Cable	330
Gas/Electric/Water	300
Fuel-Oil	0
Credit Cards	75
Insurance (Auto/Home)	260
Insurance (Life/Health)	615
Medical Bills	15
Loans/Debts	0
Transportation	0
Food/Groceries	2,000
Education	0

Clothing	100
Entertainment	80
Gasoline	300
Payroll Taxes	1,666
Pocket Money	300
Savings	900
Tithe	880
Other	
Other	
Total Expense	8,671
Net Surplus/Deficit	$129 ($8800—$8671 = $129)

Take that $129 surplus, save it in a separate enve-lope, and once you accumulate $1,000, place it in an investment for additional money for retirement or to buy your vacation home or land. Even with this surplus I am concerned about the utility expenses, especially the cable and telephone bills. I am also concerned about the insurance expenses: health, life, auto, and homeowners. I would question the amount to see if the client that I am coaching is spending excessively on these items. Maybe they could lower their auto, homeowner's, and health insurance, without compromising coverage. Or maybe the deductible is too low, which is just food for thought. These items will be discussed in separate chapters. I would be very cautious about the life insurance before making any changes or adjustments to the face amount. Life insurance is used for replacement of income and for estate planning. This will be discussed further in the insurance chapter. I know you are excited to learn more, but haste makes waste. We will get there!

I suggest that couples base the budget, using the husband's income only. There are times when the wife's income will be interrupted by a pregnancy, illness, or a change in location due to husband's employment. The wife's income can be used for special one-time purchases, like furniture, an automobile, or a second home. If you want to combine husband's and wife's income, you can, as long as you make an adjustment two to three years in advance if you know the wife's income will cease. You want to make the adjustments so your bills do not exceed your income and you are still saving and investing.

If your income exceeds your expenses, that extra money can be used for additional investing in other areas that will be discussed later when we discuss investments. A little hint, you will use the envelope system to amass additional money for maybe a vacation home or land.

Objective: when you are preparing your budget, after you tithe, you must pay yourself first and save 10–20 percent of your income each and every payday for your future retirement.

The example of the above budget will serve you well over the years to come. Now you can custom-design your own budget, and you will be on your way to financial liberty. Your budget will have to be modified as situations change in your life. That is the beautiful thing about a budget; you can change it as circumstances change in your life. Remember, numbers do not lie. The budget will help you to realize that you can trim the fat off your expenses and live more lean, but comfortable. You will be able to consummate goals that you have not been able to accomplish in the past. This will happen for you because you have taken the right step to financial independence. You are on your way.

Congratulations! I am proud of you for taking the steps needed to free yourself from financial bondage. Now you are controlling your finances, your finances are not controlling you. After a few months you will see and feel the effects that have changed your life for the better. You will have more *discretionary income* left over for investing and saving for your future. That's the key: to have more money for your future and make your future secure. You now have a plan of action, and you are in the driver's seat.

$$\text{Gross Income} - \text{Taxes} - \text{Necessities} =$$
$$\text{Discretionary Income}$$

Gross income: before any deductions to income
Taxes: federal/state/local/FICA
Necessities: food, clothing, rent/mortgage, entertainment, utilities, insurance, transportation, etc.

This is just a rule of thumb for you to follow for your finances in percentages (based on net income)

10%   tithe
10%   cash-liquidity (your emergency fund)
20%   investments—401k, IRA, stocks, mutual funds, bonds, CDs, money market, annuity, etc.
60%   what you will live on.

After your budget is in place you need to establish an ***emergency fund***. An emergency fund is exactly that, the fund is used for emergencies only. It is not used to buy an automobile, to go on a vacation, to buy a television, or the like. Do you get the picture? An emergency is when the automobile breaks down, the refrigerator needs to be repaired, job loss, you break a tooth, and so forth. An emergency fund is not a slush fund. It is only used for emergencies. That's all!

You ask, why should I waste my money on that? If something breaks, I will use current income. Maybe you can. But wouldn't you want to be certain? Or do you want to guess? Do you know how to get to work? Or do you guess how to get to work? If you are guessing how you get to work, you won't have your job for very long. Without an emergency fund, you will have to scramble for money. You may have to borrow the money, use your credit card, or take out a loan. You do not want to owe anyone money. What if you owed Uncle Sam money, what would you do? See you are still thinking! Just establish the emergency fund.

Are you still reluctant to establish an emergency fund? I know you cannot afford to establish one. Let me be straight with you, you *cannot afford* not to have one. Case in point: James has a very good position with a Fortune 500 company. He earns a six-figure income. His wife, Jane, is a school teacher, earning $40,000 per year. Jane wanted to establish an emergency fund, but James was reluctant. They have no emergency fund. Due to the economy, unfortunately, James lost his job. He has been out of work for eight months. Do you think this couple needed an emergency fund? You bet they did!

See, we never know when the calamities of life will erupt and hit us hard. It is just foolish. It's like the guy who bought a brand-new car for $45,000 but refused to insure it. His car was stolen. Too bad for him, without insurance he just lost $45,000. Can you afford to lose $45,000? I can't! The average worker can't. Neither can you! Please don't be foolish. An emergency fund is like having an insurance policy. It's there in case there is a loss. Do not procrastinate!

This is how you establish an emergency fund. You need to set aside at least 10 percent of your income until you have amassed 6–12 months of income. If your expenses are greater than your income, you are in trouble. You don't need a bandaid, you need surgery. Wants have to be eliminated immediately from your expenses. The TV has to go, Internet service has to go, excess telephones have to go, eating out has to go, lawn service has to go; whatever has to be eliminated to abate your excess expenses has to be done now. You have been living way above your means, and the insanity must stop now. Yes, now you must curtail expenses that are not biological needs or that do not impede your health.

Capisce (understand)!!!!! Come on, it's time to get with the program.

The old school of thought was to save 10 percent of income until 3–6 months of income is saved. But this is not the old days. With today's economic conditions and uncertainty, 6–12 months is a minimum. With unemployment the way it is, no one knows how long it will take to procure employment. It is better to have more saved then less. Your emergency fund has to be in a liquid asset, like a savings account or a money market account. It must be liquid. I advise you, besides having an emergency fund, you should have $1,000 in cash for unexpected events, where you need the money now and in *cash*. Take $1,000 cash, small bills and keep it readily available to you in your home for any unexpected event where you need cash immediately. These ideas and methods will help secure your future. *Please, do not ransom your future to benefit yourself today.*

There is another form I would like to share with you that you should update annually and will render a bird's-eye view of where you stand financially. The form is a *balance sheet*. A balance sheet will show you your financial position. It will list all of your *assets* and **liabilities,** which will show you how much you are really *worth*. It is a crucial tool and must be used in conjunction with your budget.

BALANCE SHEET:

Assets:

Cash Equivalents _____

Checking Accounts _____

Savings Accounts   _____

Life Insurance Cash Value   _____

Cash   _____

Miscellaneous   _____

Total: _____

Invested Assets:

Common Stock   _____

Corporate Bonds   _____

Mutual Funds   _____

Vested Pension Benefits   _____

Retirement Plans   _____

Miscellaneous Investments   _____

Rental Property   _____

Total: _____

Used Assets:

Residence   _____

Personal Property   _____

Automobile   _____

Miscellaneous   _____

Total: _____

Liabilities:

Credit Cards   _____

Automobile Loan   _____

Mortgage Balance   _____

Student Loans   _____

Personal Loans   _____

Miscellaneous   _____

Total: _____

Net Worth: _____

       _____

Formula: Assets – Liabilities = Net Worth

An individual's net worth is the amount remaining after subtracting from the sum of his assets any creditor claims against the assets. The bottom line is, it is not how many assets you own, it's how many of those assets are owned *free and clear.* That's the key, to own everything you possess *free and clear* from any debt. As you can now realize, your objective is to own everything free and clear, to buy with cash and to be totally debt-free. Being debt-free is what it is all about. I know you can do it and you will do it!

Proverbs: 21:20. In the house of the wise are the stores of choice food and oil, but the foolish man devours all he has.

The proverb is about saving for the future. Easy credit has many people living on the edge of bankruptcy. The desire to keep up and accumulate more pushes them to spend every penny they earn, and they stretch their credit to the limit. But anyone who spends all he has is spending more than he can afford. A wise person puts money aside for when he or she may have less. God approves of foresight and restraint. God's people need to examine their lifestyles to see whether their spending is God-pleasing or merely self-pleasing.

God speaks about one of His financial principals called *surety*. Surety is taking an obligation without knowing a concrete way to pay for it. God's financial principal will help you to avert the money traps set by the world's economic system. Instead of *buy now,* you must *save to buy.* This will help you not to act recklessly with your money. You must elude buying on credit because you do not know what the *future* holds. *Caution*—Do not co-sign a loan for anyone. If the person you co-signed for defaults on the loan, you become the party who is responsible for the loan.

Proverbs: 11:15. He who puts up security for another will surely suffer, but whoever refuses to strike hands in pledge is safe.

Action Plan

Action Plan

Which Credit Card Bills Do You Pay Off First?

There are many different thoughts on which credit card bills you should tackle or pay off first. During my schooling, I was exposed to two different methods in my finance class. The first took the position of listing all of your credit card bills, smallest amount owed to the largest amount owed. No problem I thought, I can do this. The instructor told us to tackle the smallest bill first and pay it off, then check it off the list as paid. What you are doing is paying off all the small amounts first, building up to paying off the larger bills last. The physiological effect was to have a good feeling that you were accomplishing, getting rid of your credit card debt. It makes sense; it is easier to pay a smaller bill off faster than paying off a larger one. I got it, I thought to myself. It makes sense. I can do it.

Then, the rhetorical question arose, what would you do if I attached an interest rate to each of those credit cards? Okay I thought, it still makes sense to pay off the smaller items first. It gives you a sense of accomplishment. So I raised my hand and told the professor what I thought. I would do the same thing. List all credit card bills, smallest to the largest; then pay the smaller bills first. It has the same effect. There was silence in the room. He walked over to me and politely said, "are you sure? Are you really sure?" I'm thinking to myself, I'm a

Bronx boy; I will not not be intimidated. So I said yes? He said let's see if you are right. Who was I to challenge a Harvard graduate working for Price Water House CPAs. After all I thought at the time that CPA stood for "can't pass arithmetic." So here came the lesson from the professor. I held on to my seat because I knew he was taking the class for a ride.

List all of your credit card bills in ranking order of the lowest interest rate to the highest interest rate and place the outstanding balance next to them. Here was his example.

$$\$1,000 @ 5\% = \$50$$
$$\$1,000 @ 10\% = \$100$$
$$\$1,000 @ 15\% = \$150$$

As you can see, the higher the interest rate the more money that credit card will cost you. His rhetorical question was, do you want to pay $50 interest or $150 in interest? Of course you want to pay the lesser of the two. Do you want to pay the $50 instead of the $150? His point was, it is always better to pay off high-interest credit cards first. The interest accumulates on the balance that is left after making your payment. Therefore, if you have a higher interest rate, you will pay more in finance charges.

His cardinal rule was never to pay the minimum on any credit card. Depending on the amount and interest rate being charged, if you pay the minimum you will be paying that bill for years to come. Paying the minimum makes no sense. This is what happens by paying the minimum: with a credit card balance of $3,000, the minimum payment is $60, the interest rate is 18.50 percent. The total payment made after eight years would be $5,760, costing you $2,760 in interest. If you paid an additional $50 per month, or a total of $110 per month, you would pay off the credit card in three years, saving five years of payments and saving yourself $1,800 in finance charges. That's your money, $1,800 for your pocket not the credit card's pocket. Take the $60 or $110 if you paid off the credit card sooner and apply this extra money to other credit cards you have to pay off. Do not take from Peter to pay Paul. Do not take cash advances to pay off another credit card debt. If you are doing this, you are living way above your means. If you are using a credit card to charge items, and you pay the balance in full at the end of the month, that's okay. If you cannot pay off the item you charged at the end of the month **do not charge.** You are living beyond your means.

If it is difficult finding extra money to pay down your debt, here are some suggestions:

*   Brown bag your lunch.

*   Car pool.

*   Make pizza at home instead of ordering out.

*   Bring your coffee to work instead of Starbucks. You will save $$$$$$.

*   If you live close to stores, run your errands by walking or riding your bike instead of using your car. It's also a lot healthier.

*   Instead of going to the movies, rent a movie and have a movie night in your home.
*   Go to Costco and buy in bulk. It is less expensive and means fewer trips to the store.

*   Change your phone and cable plans.

These are only a few suggestions. Be creative and think outside the box. If you truly want to spend your money more prudently and get out of debt, be positive and do it. Like I mentioned before, *don't ransom your future for an immediate benefit today.* Trust me, It is not worth it.

Back to my professor: even though he prefers paying off the high-interest credit cards first, he was not opposed to paying off the smaller item first. His main objective was to have you take action immediately and get it done. Whichever method you choose is fine, as long as you choose one. Do not procrastinate to put this plan into action. If you do, the consequences are catastrophic.

Just to let you know, I personally do not use credit cards unless it is absolutely necessary. If I do use a credit card, immediately the money is placed aside into the envelope so when the bill arrives it is paid immediately. There have been times that I have taken the money from the envelope and paid the bill before the statement arrives in the mail. It is all about your attitude to be debt-free and take control of your finances for your well-being.

Action Plan

Action Plan

Saving for Something Special

No matter where I am or who I am coaching, one of the most prevalent questions I am asked is, "Coach how do I save for something special?" I don't know! What are you looking to buy? The answer maybe you want to buy a new suit, a new dress, a new car, or go on a vacation. So what you are really asking is, can I save to buy something? Keep in mind, luxury versus necessity, needs versus wants. The first question to ask yourself should be, do I want it or do I need it? Next, what is the reason I want this or need this? How will it impact my life? What will this purchase do for me? Will it have a major change to my life? How will it change my life? Who will this purchase impact? Why do I need this? Where will I purchase this? How much will it cost? When am I looking to purchase this? I am simple asking the five W questions and the 1 H question. I call them the five W brothers and the one H sister. Just like in grammar school: *what, who, why, where, when,* and *how.*

This may seem elementary, and it is. But, if we don't first think elementary, we will miss the boat: financial freedom, waking up debt-free, having financial serenity, I don't care what you call it, it's all about having your financial house in order. In essence, there is nothing intricate about it. What does make it difficult, is, you were never taught the financial principles of money. Maybe no one showed you how to deal with money matters. You are not alone.

Over the past 25 years I have seen and witnessed the abuse, yes abuse, of money. So many people, whether poor, average, or rich have gotten themselves in trouble with money. Yes, even the rich have money problems. Why do you read about so many actors, boxers, baseball players, basketball players who have died broke. A boxer I followed for years earned millions of dollars, yes millions of dollars, but when he died, he died broke. His fellow boxers paid for his funeral services. That was the one an only "smokin' Joe Frazier." When I read the story in the Newspaper I was heartbroken. As I mentioned earlier, *"people don't plan to fail; they fail to plan."*

It makes no sense to buy things that you cannot afford. I have worked with people over the years that have uncontrollable spending habits. The use of the *credit card* is *devastating.* I cannot overemphasize the credit card abuse that I see while working with individuals to get their financial plan on track. You must understand that buying that item is immediate gratification. But what happens when that item is no longer gratifying you and the credit card bill arrives, and you do not have the money to pay for it in full. Finance charges begin to accumulate. You get nervous and scared; you look for other alternatives, but there are none. You borrow from family and friends. Now you can't pay them back. You cannot pay your bills! Now what? You consider bankruptcy, but it has its own issues.

Just to let you know, the banks and credit card and finance companies love people who finance. That's how they earn an abundance of money. It's okay for them to earn money; it's the entrepreneurial spirit. But their practices cripple people with their finances. Don't become a victim to the finance craze. You will lose financially.

In my accounting days I audited an auto dealership that sold used cars. I learned that the important thing that they had to do was buy used automobiles for a great price and to ascertain that the automobiles that they were buying were reliable and would not break down when they resold them. If the automobile broke down after the sale, the dealership would have to repair the auto for the first 12 months the buyer owned the car. That can become costly and cat into profits I was able to understand that. It made sense. But during the audit process I noticed that the dealership had finance charges as receivables. I inquired with the owner to explain this to me. What he told me blew me away. He said that the dealership does its own financing. Okay so far, I understand. If it was not for the financing, there would be no profit. All of the sales revenue generated covers all of the overhead and expenses. The finance charges are what yields the dealership profit. He said that we discourage people from buying automobiles in cash. We want them to finance so we can earn money. The finance charges are the dealership's profits.

Financing is big business for companies. My point is to not get dragged into the financing scheme. Financing costs money. It costs you your money—money that you cannot afford to lose. If you cannot pay cash, forget about financing to buy anything. When you finance, you are still paying for the item as it continues to age. In most cases by the time you have finished paying off the finance charges for the item you purchased, it's time for you to start the process over again because the item has become obsolete or it is desuetude.

Let me tell you about a client of mine who lives in New York. This gentleman refinances every year or two because he is spending his money on things he cannot afford. It is very easy to take out the credit card to buy, but it is very hard to pay off the bill in full when the bill arrives in the mail. I have spoken with him about his purchases, and he told me, "I need to remodel my kitchen, or, I need to remodel the bathroom, or my son needs this, or my daughter needs that, or I need money for education for the kids." The reason why he constantly refinances is because he needs to take the equity out of his house so he can pay off his high credit card debt. The problem is every time he refinances, he always starts over again. He starts from the beginning, always going back to a 30-year mortgage.

I have known this man for twenty years. As of the beginning of 2012, he has a brand new 30-year mortgage, starting from the beginning again. What a waste of money. He is always broke and constantly complains that he has no savings and no retirement plan. Not even one at work, because he refuses to contribute into his 401k Plan. By the way the employer matches up to 6 percent. He is losing **free money** from his employer. He is constantly wasting money and never getting ahead. If you cannot afford it, do not buy it. It is time for him to have plastic surgery and cut up those credits that are drowning him in debt. Stop the pain and go for the gain. Credit card debt yields **pain**, while no debt yields **gain**. There is an old adage that says you can lead the horse to water, but you can't make the horse drink, just like the individual in my above example whom I have been coaching for years. When I am not on top of him due to other obligations, he falls short. I can design the best financial program in the world, but if you do not adhere to it and heed my words you will go nowhere. The person who drives to an unknown place without a map is a fool. Take the map with you so you do not get lost. This guy is lost and drowning in financial debt. He refuses to use a road map to stay on the road to financial freedom.

Now, how do you save for something you want? Once your financial plan is in order, your house is in order. You have a budget established, all your expenses/bills are up to date, and you have established your emergency fund. In addition, you have answered the five W brothers and the one H sister questions and you have prayed on what you want to buy that is special to you. You will utilize the envelope system in which each time you get paid you will set a certain amount aside until you have amassed the required amount to make your purchase. You will not borrow any money for this purchase. You will not use credit of any kind for this purchase. You will not finance this purchase. You will only use *cash*. Cash is king, and everything you buy is negotiable—especially when you use cash.

The merchant would rather make a cash transaction because they save money. Every time a merchant accepts a credit card, it costs them money. Some of those credit cards that offer incentives and points cost the merchant big money in fees that they are charged. The credit card company/bank earns money from you, the customer, when you finance and from the merchant when you use the credit card to make a purchase. That's why the banks have all the money.

The reason why I love the envelope system so much is because when you take your hard-earned money and place it in that envelope each and every time you get paid, you will start to see it grow. That's a beautiful thing. You will see your diligence and effort being rewarded by your consistency. You will see that through patience and time, you will accumulate the money you need for your purchase. But, what you will eventually realize is not only how long it took you to accumulate that money, but also how fast you can spend it. This envelope system allows your mind to think differently and think about things you might not have thought about in the past. How large the ticket item you are looking to purchase will dictate how long it will take to amass your money for the purchase. This is called *delayed gratification!* That is a very good character trait, indeed.

Once you reach your goal, don't be surprised if you question yourself and say, "do I really need to buy that"? Now that's a beautiful thing. You will realize, "is this a need or a want." At that point in time, only you will be able to make that decision. I will not be there. You will *need* to coach yourself. That's okay! You want to be able to coach yourself. You will need to become your own teacher. *Once you can pay cash for everything, your wants will change.* It is a different mindset when you pay with cash as opposed to paying with a credit card. With cash you feel the effect instantly. But with credit, the effect is delayed and you will treat it as another bill. This is wrong, and please do not do that.

I have witnessed virtuosos tell their students that I will teach you to teach yourself. Yes, it makes sense. If the teacher is no longer there, does the student stop growing? No, the student will continue to grow on his or her own. This is my purpose, to get you to think differently and to help you to be your own coach/teacher. I want you to stand on your own and make prudent financial decisions when no one is watching you or looking over your shoulder. I will give you the keys to open the door, but you have to unlock the door and open it. Remember, integrity is making the right decisions when no one is *watching!*

Many, many times in my life I have used the envelope system, and when I accumulated the money and was ready to buy in cash, I backed down. I realized that I really did not need that item, and it was more of a want then a need. I am sure you get the picture. Make certain you are buying for the right reason. It is very difficult and takes a long time to save a large sum of money, but you can spend it in a blink of an eye. Just remember that. I want you to be good stewards of your money. I want you to be great stewards of the Lord's money.

Warnings Against Folly

Proverbs: 6:1–5. My son, if you have put up security for your neighbor, if you have struck hands in pledge for another, if you have been trapped by what you said, ensnared by the words of your mouth, then do this, my son, to free yourself, since you have fallen into your neighbor's hands: Go and humble yourself; press your plea with your neighbor! Allow no sleep to your eyes. Free yourself, like a gazelle from the hand of the hunter, like a bird from the snare of the fowler.

These verses are not a plea against generosity, but against overextending one's financial resources and acting in irresponsible ways that could lead to poverty. It is important to maintain a balance between generosity and good stewardship. God wants us to help our friends and the needy, but he does not promise to cover the costs of every unwise commitment we make. We should also act responsibly so that our family does not suffer. What I relish so much about this proverb is that we should be great stewards of God's money, but also not to be unwise with the use of our money and to act responsible so our family does not suffer. That's the key, to act *responsibly* with money. Webster's definition of responsible is: answerable, able to distinguish from right and wrong, involving obligations or duties. Do the right thing and be responsible with your hard-earned money.

Take a piece of paper, write "responsible with God's money," and place it where you will see and read it each and every day. You must be accountable for your actions with the money you earn and act responsibly when spending it.

Action Plan

Action Plan

INSURANCE

*D*uring this section we will discuss the different types of insurance and their purpose and applicability in your financial plan. First, let's discuss what insurance truly means; insurance is the transfer of risk from one institution to another. You as an individual will transfer your risk or loss exposure by making a premium payment to an insurance company where the insurance company will set aside a pool of money to protect your exposure or risk. Many individuals cannot afford to self-insure. Even the affluent who can self-insure still own various kinds of insurance to protect their loss exposure and risk for pennies on the dollar. Just to let you know, even the individuals who can self-insure realize that it is prudent for them to own various kinds of insurance. It is a prudent decision to transfer the risk. See, if we knew when a loss would occur, we would buy insurance right before the loss occurred. But of course we do not know when a loss will occur. Therefore, act intelligently.

There are many different kinds of insurance which we will discuss throughout this section. We will also discuss the reason for these different kinds of insurance and their purpose in your life. Insurance is an integral part of a comprehensive and strong financial plan. As we say in the financial planning world, insurance is part of the financial triangle and creates a solid financial foundation. A note to take is that a structure (house, building) has to be built on a solid foundation or during the first storm the structure will collapse. You do not want your financial plan to collapse, because your financial plan is not on solid ground.

Insurance is replacement of money due to a financial loss. Any kind of financial loss is taxing on a financial plan. It takes a long time, years, to build wealth, and it can be wiped out in the blink of an eye. You do not want to lose all of the years you worked to amass your wealth, and lose it quickly, because you failed to protect all of your assets, including your human asset value. Let me give it to you straight, no matter who you are, where you live, who you know, who you don't know, whatever, you will be confronted with some kind of risk. Everyone has an exposure. It could be a health issue that will drain your pocket book without the proper insurance in place. Or maybe you had an accident with your automobile and you did not have enough coverage to defray the lawsuit or medical bills you are now responsible for. Or the breadwinner in the family has become disabled or even worse, a loss of life, leaving the family without income.

What would you or your family do, if you were confronted with one of the above situations? It is a very frightening feeling to have no income due to a disability, loss of income, or to the loss of the breadwinner. Imagine waking up every morning with no income. Think about that, with no income coming into the household each and every day, the bills would pile up. There would be no money to buy food and no money to pay for any of those bills piling up. It is a very scary situation to be in. Please do not put yourself or your family in this very perilous situation. Your life as well as your family's life would be discombobulated and confused. There is absolutely no reason to ever place yourself and your family's life in uncharted waters when there are steps you can take to thwart this from happening.

Remember, we will not know ahead of time when the calamities of life will hit us, and it will hit us hard. I cannot overemphasize the point of proper protection. Do not be penny wise and dollar foolish. Don't be one of those people who say, " I wish I would have done this or that," or "I wish I would have only listened." Don't do that to yourself. Your decisions affect others too. It's not just about you. You know better and must act responsible. It is your obligation as the leader of your home to protect your family against the calamities of life and provide for your family. There are no excuses!

1 Timothy 5:8. If anyone does not provide for his relatives, and especially for his immediate family, he has denied the faith and is worse than an unbeliever.

Paul says, that a person who neglects his or her family responsibilities has denied the faith. Are you doing your part to meet the needs of those included in your family circle?

During the next several chapters we will discuss and uncover the need and purpose of various kinds of insurance. We will take a closer look at:

- Life Insurance
- Health Insurance—Major Medical
- Disability Insurance
- Homeowner's Insurance
- Auto Insurance
- Liability Insurance

These insurances listed above will help you build your solid financial foundation. This foundation will help you to go forward and place you in a better and stronger financial position. Ask yourself, is it important to be financially secure and be able to weather the **STORM?** If you answered yes, it is time to understand and begin building your solid financial foundation. Insurance replaces the uncertainty of risk with guarantees. The most effective way of managing risk is to *transfer* it, so that the loss is borne by another party.

Action Plan

_____
_____
_____
_____
_____
_____
_____
_____
_____
_____
_____
_____
_____
_____
_____
_____
_____
_____
_____
_____
_____
_____
_____
_____
_____
_____
_____
_____
_____
_____
_____
_____
_____

Action Plan

Life Insurance

To better understand the purpose and function of life insurance one has to understand the *Human Asset Value.* The Human Asset Value has an individual monetary value to those who depend on him or her. This can either be the breadwinner in a household or a key employee(s) or owner(s) in a business. There is also a monetary value placed on a business or key individuals in a business that needs to be protected. We will discuss this later. For now let's just keep it simple.

The Human Asset Value can be measured by an individual's future earnings. It is the ability for a family to exist and pay for all their bills: education, home purchase, retirement savings, and so forth. In essence, it is an individual's or family's economic existence. A person's value is subject to the loss through death or retirement. It is for this purpose that the human life value has to be conserved and protected. That's why life insurance exits.

Here is a chart for you to detect what your *Human Asset Value* is. This chart is to make you realize your earning power and potential. Many people do not have any clue to the amount of money they will generate over a lifetime. Now you will be able to have a bird's-eye view of seeing what amount of money you can earn over your lifetime. You will say, *"Wow, that is a lot of Escarole!"* as we say in the old country of Italy. You will unequivocally earn a fortune over your lifetime. But the important questions are: What will you do with your money? How will you protect your earning power? To make it more apparent and meaningful, you are a money-making machine. Protect that machine against the risks of life. There are only two ways to earn money; people earn money and money earns money. That's it! So protect the money-making machine, *yourself!*

As I mentioned earlier in the book, it is up to you, if you want a *future that is certain and secure.* Follow the plan, stick with it; it works!

Let's now take a look at the chart below to see what your earning potential is. If your number is not in the chart, be creative and think outside the box. If your income is $200,000 per year, then multiply the $100,000 by two and all the applicable numbers in the columns. If your income is $15,000 per year, divide the $30,000 by two and all the applicable numbers in the columns to derive at your numbers. The chart is to give you an idea of how much money you will earn over a lifetime. You will be amazed.

You'll earn a fortune over your lifetime.

YEARS TO RETIREMENT

Annual Salary	35 Years		30 Years		25 Years		20 Years	
	S	A	S	A	S	A	S	A
100000	3500000	9032000	3000000	6644000	2500000	4772000	2000000	3306000
90000	3150000	8129000	2700000	5979000	2250000	4296000	1800000	2979000
80000	2800000	7226000	2400000	5316000	2000000	3818000	1600000	2646000
70000	2450000	6322000	2100000	4651000	1750000	3341000	1400000	2315000
60000	2100000	5419000	1800000	3986000	1500000	2864000	1200000	1984000
50000	1750000	4516000	1500000	3322000	1250000	2386000	1000000	1653000
40000	1400000	3613000	1200000	2658000	1000000	1909000	800000	1323000
30000	1050000	2710000	900000	1993000	750000	1432000	600000	992000

S - Straight Projections: Total earnings until retirement assuming no increases.

A - Adjusted Projections: Total earnings until retirement assuming a 5% annual Increase.

Income you will earn over a lifetime. Just find yourself on the chart.

Ideally you should be setting aside at least 10%-15% of your paycheck to provide for your future needs.

Just imagine yourself with the right financial plan and what you can amass from your income. You just have to have the right attitude, the willingness to listen, and then take action immediately without any procrastination. The most difficult thing for people to do is to take action. I encourage you to take action now and begin to place yourself and your family in a better and stronger financial position. You and your family deserve it.

Life insurance is not only used to replace income in case of premature death, but also used to supplement a retirement. If an individual, called the *insured* has permanent insurance, like whole life, that insurance can be used to supplement retirement income by using the cash value of the life insurance. As an individual starts out in life their insurance needs will not be as great as when they start a family, buy a home, invest in a business, and so forth, their insurance needs will increase. There are times when an individual is nearing retirement that their life insurance needs will decrease. At that time, if they have permanent life insurance like whole life, they can use the cash value in the policy for retirement. They can either take the money in cash or have the insurance company create an annuity, which can be a steady stream of monthly income. Who wouldn't want that?

As we approach retirement, sometimes our need for life insurance does not decrease, but increases due to an estate that has grown in size and life insurance is used to protect that asset. It all depends on the individual's situation. Life insurance is not one-size-fits-all. Life insurance is a personal decision and used to protect income.

Types of Life Insurance Companies:

Stock Insurers—The stockholders own the company. Stockholders may or may not be policyholders. When the company pays a dividend, it goes to the stockholders.

Mutual Insurers—Any person buying insurance from a mutual company is considered the owner. The company is owned by the policyholders, not the stockholders. If the company is participating, when the company declares a dividend, the dividend goes to the policyholders. A dividend is an annual return of premiums in excess of those needed to cover current costs. The policy is called participating.

There are many different purposes for life insurance. Here are some of the reasons for the use of life insurance. Replacement of monthly income, final expense fund, housing fund, education fund, dependency period, blackout period, money needed for a special needs individual, retirement income, and estate planning, are just some of the uses of life insurance. Even though there are many different kinds of insurance on the market today, to keep things simple, it still comes down to just two different kinds, term and permanent. Remember one size doesn't fit all.

There are many people out there today that profess that you should buy term insurance and invest the difference. *I do not agree.* I have a sincere problem with that kind of provincial thinking. First of all, the majority of people who buy term **do not** invest the difference. Second, for those who do invest, the majority do not know where to invest and do not monitor their investment. Third, without performing a needs analysis and asking relevant questions, how can someone tell you to just buy term. They can't; whoever tells you that is just making a blanket statement. Those individuals are guiding you and many others the wrong way and shame on them. I will explain to you when term insurance should be used and when permanent insurance, like whole life should be used. I will explain this to you, and you will know when to use term versus permanent life insurance.

Let me tell you a story about myself. I have gone against the grain of all those who say to buy term and invest the difference. I own all whole life insurance that pays dividends. When I did have a mortgage, the only term insurance that I owned was to cover my outstanding mortgage balance. The reason why I did not have whole life to cover the mortgage balance was because I was just starting out and could not afford the whole life. But as my pay increased, I converted the term to a whole life insurance policy and ended up paying off a 30-year mortgage in 10 years by using the cash value in the policy, plus using money I amassed on the side in the envelope system. Those whole life policies that were dividend-paying helped me to buy my wife a Chrysler van in 1997. Those dividend paying policies also helped me to defray my children's college expenses. In addition, when the market crashed and everyone's 401k became a 201k, my whole life dividend-paying policies were still paying dividends and helped me to increase my wealth.

This is the economic values of *permanent life insurance.* "Few things in life are certain and nothing in life is permanent except change. The unique benefit of life insurance is that it protects against the uncertainties and changes in life. It provides cash to the insured in times of emergencies or to the insured's beneficiaries in the event of death. The life insurance contract creates assets with the stroke of a pen. An immediate estate is created by life insurance. No bond, savings account, real estate, stock, or mutual fund can provide an instant estate with only a fraction of its ultimate value as a down payment."

Life Underwriter Training Council Course, volume1 1983 edition, page 31.

My point is this, do not dismiss permanent life insurance like whole life insurance. There is unequivocally a place for permanent insurance, and it should not be dismissed. Before you buy any kind of life insurance, you need to determine what the reason(s) for the insurance is. Only then, can you determine what type of insurance is appropriate for you.

What type of life insurance should be used depends on the situation. Let's discuss what term insurance is. *Term insurance* is the simplest form of life insurance. It provides protection only as a death benefit; it has no cash value and offers no living benefits that are associated with permanent insurance. Term insurance is temporary insurance, which is used to cover a temporary need. It provides coverage for only a temporary period of time. Once the period of time expires, the insurance comes to an end. Remember term insurance if for a specific period of time and expires when that time arrives. That's why you have to be very careful to determine what type of insurance is appropriate and right for you and your family. You do not want your insurance to expire when you need it most. Imagine that your insurance expired on October 1, 2012, and unfortunately you died on October 2, 2012. What would you family do without you and without your income? It would be a traumatic experience for your family to experience. Your income is lost due to your demise, and now your family is scrambling about how they are going to exist without your income. The bills are piling up due to the loss of your income. Only life insurance for pennies on the dollar can replace your income. The same holds true for the loss of a man's spouse. The woman also has a human asset value, regardless if she works or not. She also must be protected.

Term insurance is like renting an apartment. You rent the apartment for a period of time, and when that period ends you either renew the contract, which will cost you more in monthly rent, or you move out and leave the apartment. Now you have to search for another apartment to live in or you buy a home, or you do nothing and live on the street. The same is true with life insurance, you either renew the term insurance and pay more premium or you decide to buy permanent insurance, or you decide to do nothing and now you have no life insurance.

The best way I can explain term insurance is through this example. You and your family are renting an apartment on Morris Park Ave in the Bronx, New York. The landlord tells you that the rental payment is $1,000 per month. For this example we will not include any rental increases. So you rent the apartment for ten years. After the ten years you tell the landlord you are moving out. You explain to the landlord that you have made your rental payments on time, you were a good tenant, and that you even made improvements to the apartment. You also tell him that you paid him $120,000 over ten years and that you want to know how much of your $120,000 you are getting back. Unfortunately for you, he tells you nothing, zero. The landlord tells you that he allowed you to live in his apartment for ten years and that is it. It is sad, but it is true. That is what will happen with term insurance. Just know what you are doing.

Term insurance provides coverage for a specified amount of time. There are 1, 5, 10, 20, 25, or 30 year policies or even term insurance to ages 65, 75, or 95, depending on what the particular insurance company offers. No matter what the number of years you select to purchase, eventually the term insurance will end. When the term insurance ends you do have the option to renew the insurance at your attained age or convert the insurance without providing evidence of insurability. As long as the contract states that you do not have to show evidence of insurability, you can renew the insurance policy at your attained age without a medical exam. If you have to obtain a medical exam to renew or convert the insurance policy, you will have to pass a medical exam to show evidence of insurability before the insurance policy is renewed or converted to a permanent insurance policy. There may even be some companies that still offer a DT-65, which is a decreasing term insurance. The life insurance remains level for three years, then starts to decrease each year until it ends at age 65.

For all practical purposes, the majority of life insurance companies that offer term insurance, upon renewal or conversion of the life insurance policy, your insurability is protected and you will not have to take a medical exam. Let's clarify the reason why in some cases you will have to show evidence of insurability and other times you do not. If you purchase renewable and convertible term insurance your evidence of insurability is protected, no medical is required upon renewal or conversion of the term insurance. If you purchase a nonrenewable and nonconvertible term policy you will have to prove evidence of insurability in order to renew or convert the term insurance. Renewable term is more expensive because as you get older, the greater the risk is to the insurance company. Older policy owners must pay higher premiums than younger policy owners.

A common type of renewable term insurance is annually renewable term (ART). This is the most basic form of life insurance. It provides coverage for one year and allows the policy owner to renew the policy each year without evidence of insurability. Each year the insurance premium increases because the insured is one year older. The premium increases are disclosed in the insurance policy. You will know at any given point of time what the new increased premium will be. All renewals or conversions must be done before the term of the insurance expires. If the insurance expires, you will need to provide evidence of insurability in order to obtain insurance. At that point if your health has declined dramatically you could be uninsurable and will not be able to purchase any type or kind of insurance.

The two principal advantages of convertible term policies are that:

1. They may be converted to permanent insurance.
2. No evidence of insurability is required when the insured executes the conversion option.

Let's take a look at the cost of term insurance.

Sample Annual Rates

Age	Insurance Amount	Annual Premium
30	$1,000,000	$240.00
35	$1,000,000	$252.00
40	$1,000,000	$336.00
45	$1,000,000	$540.00
50	$1,000,000	$804.00
55	$1,000,000	$1,224.00
60	$1,000,000	$1,788.00

These figures are from *Kiplinger's Personal Finance Magazine*, October 2012

The sample above is based on a 10-year California best class female term life premiums and are not specific to any individual or insurer. (Life Quotes, Inc).

Here is another example of term insurance

Sample Annual Rates

Age	Term of Insurance	Insurance Amount	Annual Premium
40	ART	$500,000	$170.00
40	10 Year	$500,000	$240.00
40	15 Year	$500,000	$295.00
40	20 Year	$500,000	$390.00
40	30 Year	$500,000	$635.00

These figures are based on a male, nonsmoker, Preferred Plus—Anico Signature Term. Premium rates derived from Compulife software as of July 2, 2012. The above information was derived from *Life Insurance Selling Magazine*, August 2012. These premiums are based on the best rates available for the examples shown. Your premiums could be different. These are only examples to show you how term insurance in the early years is cost effective for younger people, but the rate increases as you get older for the same amount of insurance coverage. These examples also disclose that the longer the term of insurance is kept, the cost of the term insurance is more expensive.

This is the term policy of a lady that I just started to coach as of September 2012. She is a female, aged 56, nonsmoker, who had a policy with the face amount of $350,000 and a term period of 15 years, with an annual premium of $919.00 for years 1–15. The insurance was purchased to leave money for her children. She does not have many assets or money to leave her two children, so she chose to buy insurance to satisfy that need. I have to commend her for thinking about her two children to leave them some money upon her demise. I love it! But here is the problem. The agent who sold her this policy did not think about the future. This lady is in good health today. Who knows if she will be in good health tomorrow. If she does not die by the age of 71, her children will not receive the $350,000 insurance. You ask why? Please let me explain.

The $919.00 she is paying annually will skyrocket to an amazing $13,617.00 annually and just keep ascending into outer space. She will never be able to afford those new premiums. This is why for her situation she got a raw deal. But she still needs and wants the insurance.

Look at this!

Policy Year	Age of Insured	Annual Cost of Insurance	Insurance Amount
16	72	$13,617.00	$350,000
17	73	$14,919.00	$350,000
18	74	$16,340.00	$350,000
19	75	$17,915.00	$350,000
20	76	$19,644.00	$350,000
25	81	$31,565.00	$350,000

There is no reason to go on and on, the premiums become ludicrous. Who would be able to afford those premiums? This lady's dreams are shattered because she was told to buy the wrong product. No one can predict when someone will die. What does she do? She can paid the absurd premiums, reduce the face amount, or go without the insurance.

Caveat Emptor—let the buyer beware. I just want you to understand what term insurance really is. It' just insurance for a specific period of time.

Let's take a look at some uses for term insurance: (advantages)

- Protection for the outstanding loan amount on your mortgage, example: A 30-year mortgage. Use a 30-year term insurance policy to protect the mortgage. After the mortgage is paid off in 30 years, the insurance will also end.

- Education Funding—Using term insurance to protect the income that is paying for the college tuition of each student. If you need to protect your income for four years or eight years, you can purchase term insurance to cover that need. If income ceases due to a premature death, the insurance will continue to pay for the tuition until the term ends.

- A young family starting out that needs income replacement but cannot afford the premium of permanent insurance due to lack of income. Term insurance is appropriate in this situation, because it is affordable and you will be able to cover and protect the majority if not all of the income. But this insurance has to be monitored so that when the insured earns more money and can afford permanent protection, he or she will begin to convert the term insurance to permanent insurance.

- Protection for a consumer loan or an auto loan, for 4 years, 5 years, whatever. The insurance is for a specific period of time. When the loan is paid off, the insurance is no longer needed. This is only an example. Do not borrow, use cash!

Just make certain that the insurance is earmarked for the specific purpose it was intended.

As you can see from the above examples, term insurance was used for a **temporary need**. Term insurance will also protect one's evidence of **insurability** if the insurance is renewable. That is a great feature of term insurance, especially if the insured's health becomes impaired. If the insured's health is impaired, you have the option to convert to a permanent plan where you will never lose the insurance as long as the premium is paid.

Every situation is different and each situation has to be taken on an individual bases. As I mentioned earlier, *there is no-one-size-fits-all*. Before you decide to buy life insurance, you need to determine how much you need and what the purpose of the life insurance is. Although there are appropriate uses for term insurance, it is important to note that the purchase of term insurance presents some dangers that are frequently overlooked and should be considered. The premium for the term contract is very low in the early years, but it becomes very expensive in the later years just as we illustrated earlier. In the later years, even if your mortgage is paid off, your kids are done with school, your kids have moved out of your home, all of your debts are paid off, you don't need any replacement of income, if that is true, which most likely it isn't. What about **final expenses**? You will still need some kind of life insurance for your final expenses. Final expenses are not limited to; outstanding mortgage balance, rent payments, any outstanding loans, medical expenses, hospital expenses, funeral expenses, estate taxes, real estate taxes, income taxes, legal expenses, and so on. Final expenses are any expenses that are left behind by the deceased.

The group insurance you have at work is term insurance. It will stay with you until you leave that employer. When you leave an employer, you have 30 days to convert the term insurance into permanent insurance. If you still need that additional coverage, it is a good idea to convert the insurance because you won't have to prove evidence of insurability. By the way, you could never have too much life insurance. In all my years in insurance, I never had widow/widower tell me that the check I was delivering was too much. The normal response is, "is that all?"

Case in point: in 1983 when I first went into the insurance business, one of my clients purchased a $250,000 whole life policy. To my dismay, in the spring of 1984 his wife had called me to tell me that her husband had just passed away. I went to her home and consoled her, completed the necessary paperwork and helped her with the funeral arrangements. When the check was issued I made arrangements to deliver the $250,000 check to her. When I presented the check to her, she was very grateful for the $250,000 but she wanted more. My point is, when it comes to life insurance (replacement of money) the majority of people can always use more. You can never have too much. Life insurance replaces money, and no one I know refuses money.

Life insurance allows the family that is left behind to live with dignity. The family does not have to be uprooted and live in a substandard way just because the breadwinner's income ceased due to a premature death. Life insurance allows the family to stay in their home and remain living in the same neighborhood, the children will attend the same schools and life will go on without any financial interruption. *That is the power of life insurance.* There is no other investment like *life insurance,* that for pennies on the dollar you can replace a breadwinner's income when the breadwinner dies. As we say in my old neighborhood in The Bronx, New York. That's a beautiful thing!

Now let's discuss *Permanent Life Insurance,* the different types and their purpose. There are many different types of permanent Life Insurance available in the market place today. The main thing to remember is permanent Life Insurance means permanent, it *will* stay with you until you *die.* That is the main objective of permanent life insurance, you can not **outlive** it, it will be there when you family **needs** it most. It does **not** expire, it *does not* have to be renewed, there is nothing to convert. Plain and simple, the permanent life insurance will remain in force as long as you continue to pay the premiums. Due to the increase in life expectancy of people, for many companies that offer permanent life insurance, the coverage remains in effect until age 121, not just age 100.

Let look at some of the permanent life insurance plans that insurance companies offer.

Whole Life—builds cash value and pays dividends if the company is participating. Offers *guaranteed cash value.* I have seen guarantees from 3 to 4 percent. If the policy pays dividends, the dividends can be used to pay for the premiums, either in part or in whole. It depends what the amount of dividends are compared to the annual premium.

Universal Life—your investment is interest sensitive, it builds cash value. You can have a level death benefit which will be equal to the face amount, or a variable death benefit which will grow over time. Universal life allows the policy owner to use the interest in the policy to pay for premiums.

Variable Universal Life—features like the universal life, except you have subaccounts where you can be invested in mutual funds. It offers level and variable death benefits.

Universal and Variable Universal Life policies allow you to put unscheduled premium payments into the plan, thereby increasing your cash value. In this type of plan there is potential for more growth but it also takes on more risk for the policyholder.

Indexed Universal Life—this type of plan is usually tied to the S&P 500. It allows you potential growth while protecting you from market losses. It has guaranteed death benefit and builds cash value.

Survivorship Life—also known as Second to Die Insurance, it covers the life of two people and pays benefits only after both people have died. It is often used by couples for estate-planning purposes, and it is typically cheaper than purchasing separate policies for each spouse.

Twenty-Year Pay Whole Life—same benefits as a whole life policy except you make premium payments for 20 years, but you are protected for your whole life. The premiums are higher because you are paying for the policy in a shorter period of time. But once it's paid, it's paid, and the cash value continues to grow.

Life to Age 65—same benefits as a whole life policy or a 20-year paid life policy except you make premium payments until age 65.

There are probably many other types of permanent insurance policies in the marketplace today. Each one has a different twist. The reason for this is to attract and accommodate different people's taste. It's like buying a regular pizza and now you want to put pepperoni on it, or extra cheese, or peppers, or chicken. Even with all of those different toppings underneath it's still pizza. The same is true with the examples I gave you, it's ***permanent insurance.*** Permanent insurance will last for your lifetime. You cannot outlive permanent insurance. As long as the premiums are paid, the insurance will be there always.

I know some of you are thinking what happens if I outlive the insurance. If I live past age 121, that's no problem! Let's say your face amount on the policy is $500,000. At age 121 when the policy endows, the face amount of the policy will be paid to you in cash. The reason for this is, at age 121, the cash value at least equals or exceeds the face amount. Therefore the company will pay the higher of the two figures. All permanent life insurance policies must mature, or endow, and pay out at the end of the life of the policy. So all that protection that you needed during your lifetime cost you nothing because you are getting it all back. The insurance company is giving you back the money because it's your money with interest. That's a beautiful thing!

Here are some policy *options and riders* to consider with your permanent life insurance.

Option to purchase additional insurance (OPAI)—it allows the insured to buy additional insurance at certain intervals without evidence of insurability. That means your insurability is protected in case you are uninsurable and need more insurance.

Waiver of Premium—it provides a valuable added security for policy owners. It pays your insurance premium in the event the insured is disabled and unable to work. Usually there is a six month waiting period before the waiver of premium is effective. After the six month waiting period, the insurance company will reimburse the six month premiums you paid and then pay your policy until age 65 if you are still disabled. Imagine having a $500,000 whole life policy with waiver of premium option. You become disabled, your premiums are waived, and at age 65 you don't need the insurance anymore so you request the cash value of the policy. In reality, you did not pay for those premiums that were waived, but you received the benefit. That's a lot of free money in your pocket.

True story: one of my former clients took out a whole life policy with me in 1983. I took the application with the first month's premium payment. The premium was $150.00 per month; the insurance coverage was $110,000. When the policy was issued, I delivered the policy to the insured. The insured became disabled at work. I completed all the paperwork and submitted the forms. He was approved by the company for being disabled. The six months elapsed, and he was still disabled. The insurance company returned the six months of premium to the insured and started to pay the $150.00 premium for the insured each and every month. Unfortunately, the insured was still disabled and never returned to work. The insurance company paid the insurance until age 65. At that time, the insured no longer needed the $110,000 of coverage. He took a reduced paid-up policy for $25,000. That is the amount he and his wife agreed on. The other $85,000 of insurance he did not need; it became null and void. The insurance company sent him a check for more than $100,000. That's the power of permanent life insurance with wavier of premium. He really received free insurance and free money. He paid nothing for this insurance.

This is an example of the power of permanent insurance. Depending on your age, amount of insurance, premium payment and type of permanent insurance, your outcome will be different. But the same principal holds true with the power of permanent life insurance.

Back to the *options and riders.*

Accidental Death Benefit Rider—If the insured dies in an accident the insurance company will pay double indemnity, two times the face amount. In other words, if the face amount is $100,000 and insured dies in an auto accident, the insurance company pays $200,000.

Living Needs Benefit—If the insured becomes terminally ill, the insurance company will allow the insured to take a percentage of the face amount while the insured is still alive to die with dignity. The insured can spend it on whatever he or she chooses to. The percentage varies by company. For this to be effective the insured must be diagnosed to die within 12 months.

I am sure there are a host of other options and riders you can look into to determine which ones are right for you. As of this writing, the only rider that can be placed on a term insurance policy is the waiver of premium. All the other options and riders I mentioned can be added to permanent insurance. All life insurance policies have a grace period, which is usually 31days to make your premium payment. Do not play with the grace period. You should make you premium payment either annually or by check draft. You want to make certain your life insurance policy does not lapse. If it lapses because of nonpayment, you will lose the coverage. That's why it's not a bad idea to insert an automatic premium loan (APL) to keep the insurance in effect. That is only available on permanent Insurance.

If you are fortunate to purchase a whole life policy that pays dividends you will have five options to choose from:

1. Dividends to buy additional insurance—called PUA's.
2. Dividends to accumulate at interest—you are earning money on your dividends.
3. Dividends used to reduce your premium payment.
4. Dividends to pay you cash.
5. Dividends to buy one year of term insurance.

Here is a secret about dividend paying policies. When the annual dividend exceeds the annual premium each and every year, you can abbreviate the policy. In the 80s and 90s, I saw policies that were projected to pay for themselves in 8–10 years. But the dividend scale today has been reduced due to economic conditions. But there are still policies today that will abbreviate, pay for themselves in 19-20 years, by using the annual dividend. It's still a beautiful thing! It depends on the insurance company, your age, amount of insurance, profitability of the company, and so forth. There are different factors that determine the dividends a company pays to its policyholders.

There is something else I would like to discuss with you concerning permanent insurance. The non-forfeiture options are important and need to be addressed. There are three options and they only apply to permanent insurance.

1. Surrender the policy and get its cash value.
2. The cash value in the policy will buy reduced paid-up insurance. That means that no premiums will be required to be paid and whatever cash value is in the policy will buy a reduced amount of insurance.
3. The cash value in the policy will buy extended term insurance. This term insurance will last as long as

the cash value lasts. For example $100,000 of insurance, which now would be considered term insurance, may last six years and 209 days. After that period expires, the insurance ends. These options are only available with permanent insurance.

There are many uses for permanent insurance, but the main focus here is to stay on a personal basis, not a business or corporate basis. There are many, many uses and advantages for utilizing permanent insurance in a business situation. This will not be discussed in this book. The purpose of this chapter is for individuals to have a clear understanding for the uses of life insurance. To understand differences between term insurance and permanent insurance, and to discern when to use which one, I want to give you a very clear picture to the true meaning of permanent life insurance through this example:

SITUATION WANTED

Please consider this my application for a job. Although I'm a strong, healthy adult and will do an adult job, I ask only a child's wage. I'll work for about $25.00 a week, and if you give me the job, I'll stay on it as long as you need me. I'll agree never to ask for a raise—in fact, I would not accept an increase even though you might consider me entitled to one. I'm thrifty, and will promise to set aside the biggest part of my salary. I'll also promise that, if you are ever hard-pressed, I'll loan you all of my cash accumulations.

Here is the job I'll do for you. If you should die prematurely, I'll help watch over your family and take good care of them, buy shoes and clothes and school books, pay the rent and grocery bills, buy all the toys and sports equipment your children can put to use, and help them all through school and get them off to a good start in their adult life. In addition, I'll promise that your family will have most of the comforts of life.

At Christmas, I'll help bring Santa Claus to your house and provide the things that bring happiness to little children. In fact, I'll try to do all the things you would do if you were here. Of course, I can't be with your children, but I'll send along memories of a thoughtful and devoted mom or dad, instead.

After the children are grown, if you don't need my services any longer, you can stop my pay and I'll say to you, "That's all right, Boss—I've enjoyed working for you all these years. Now to show my appreciation, I'll provide you and your spouse a retirement income for the rest of your lives." All these things I'll do for you—and all I ask is that you put me on the payroll for $25.00 a week.

That's the true value and benefit of permanent life insurance. There is nothing else to say!!!

This story was taken from the Life Underwriter Training Council Course, volume 2, 1983 Edition.

Some Examples for the Use of Cash Value Life Insurance:

- Education—private school, college (cash value can be used)
- Final Expenses—burial expenses, remaining bills, medical bills, etc.
- Shelter—rental expense (cash value can be used)
- Emergencies—unexpected expenses (cash value can be used)
- Mortgage—loan on your home (can use cash value to prepay loan amount)
- Monthly Income—replacement of income due to a premature death or disability
- Supplementing Retirement Income—additional money for retirement

- Special Needs Child/Disabilities—money to take care of this child after your demise or during your living years(can use cash value)
- Home Purchases—money for down payment
- Business Opportunities—money for business investment

These are just some of the uses of life insurance. There are many, many more uses of life insurance, you just have to be creative. Term insurance can only be used for some of the above examples, while permanent insurance can be used for all of the above examples. Just think outside the box.

All life insurance proceeds, term insurance, permanent insurance are paid to a named beneficiary tax-free. One last note: do not make a minor a beneficiary. Do you think a minor will know how to deal with $500,000 or even $100,000? Of course not! I know adults who do not know how to deal with a windfall of $50,000. Plus, no insurance company is going to release money to a minor. You will just create problems for your loved ones. We will discuss this further in the estate planning section.

To determine an exact amount of life insurance that is needed to replace income, you will have to decide how much income you want to replace and for how long. You may also want to include some other items like paying off outstanding debt, paying off a mortgage balance, providing for educational needs, final expenses, and so on. It is best to sit with an insurance professional who will conduct a needs analysis for your individual situation and tailor design a program that fits your needs and budget. As a rule of thumb, a minimum of ten times your income is a guide when using life insurance as income replacement. Keep in mind what happened on September 11, 2001. After that awful tragedy, there was talk that income replacement had to be closer to twenty times income. These are just guidelines.

Action Plan

Action Plan

HEALTH INSURANCE

*P*rotect your financial security with health insurance. Most people don't plan their health insurance. They either don't have enough coverage or don't have the proper coverage. The importance of health insurance just like other types of insurance is to transfer your risk and to limit your financial exposure. It is extremely important to select the proper coverage for you and your family. Many people are able to purchase health insurance through their employer, which helps to defray the cost. Some people have to buy health insurance on their own and have to defray the entire cost. Health insurance covers the cost of the insured's medical and surgical expenses. Depending on the type of health insurance determines if the insured has to pay the costs of medical treatment out of their pocket and then be reimbursed or the insurer makes payments directly to the provider.

Everybody at some point in their life will need medical attention to some degree. You don't want to get caught unprepared. Medical expenses are very costly and without the proper coverage could bring financial disaster on a family. Your entire savings could be wiped out do to a medical emergency. Twenty to thirty years of savings can vanish due to no medical coverage or the wrong type of coverage. It is imperative to know your medical coverage from your provider and understand it. For those of you who are familiar with the movie *John Q* with Denzel Washington. He thought he had the proper coverage, but found out differently when his son got sick and needed a heart transplant. He sold everything he owned and still did not have enough money for the heart transplant for his son. Be careful, make sure you are properly insured and understand what you have. You should review your coverage from your provider at least annually.

Since the 1990s millions of U.S. citizens have found themselves with absolutely no health insurance. Don't be one of them!

These are five types of health insurance plans in the United States (as of this writing):

1. Managed Care Plans—are health insurance plans that have a contract with health care providers and medical care facilities to provide medical care at special prices. Usually the costs are lower. These providers form a network of doctors and hospitals. The network has rules which stipulate how much of the care the plan will pay for.

2. Indemnity Plans—The insured can choose any doctor he or she wants. The doctor, the hospital or the insured submits a claim for reimbursement to the health insurance company. It is vital to read the benefits summary page to understand when you are entitled to be reimbursed. Indemnity plans do not typically pay 100 percent of the cost. They usually pay 80 percent of the medical and surgical services, while the insured (you) pay the other 20 percent. This 80/20 split is called coinsurance. The insured is also responsible for any excess chargers that the doctor chargers that are in excess of what is considered reasonable or customary. For example: the customer fee for high blood pressure is $200, the doctor charges

$250. The insurance company pays $160 (200 x 80%) You pay $40 (200 x 20%) plus $50 (250 – 200) for a total amount of $90 (40 + 50). There is also a deductible that has to be paid before the reimbursement kicks in. This is an out of pocket maximum within a 12-month period that the insured has to meet before the insurance provider pays 100 percent.

In addition, the insurance company will only pay up to the maximum lifetime benefit. If the maximum lifetime benefit is $2 million, the insurance company will pay benefits until the $2 million has been reached.

3. Health Maintenance Organization (HMO)—The insured goes directly to the HMO medical provider to see health care professionals. The insured does not pay for each individual service. A set premium is paid to the HMO, which in return offers a variety of services which includes preventive care. If you need to see a specialist, you have to first see your primary care physician who will refer you to a specialist in the network. All of the medical specialists in the network can only charge a certain fee for services because these fees have already been negotiated by the HMO. This keeps the cost to a minimum. HMOs are the least expensive of the plans offered. In most cases there will also be a co pay that the insured has to pay.

4. Preferred Provider Organization—A PPO is like a indemnity plan; the insured can see any doctor he or she chooses whenever they want to. The PPO negotiates preferential prices with the health care providers, health professionals and laboratories. The providers that come to agreed deals with the PPO become part of the network. There are co-payments and deductibles.

5. Point of Service Plans—A POS Plan is like a hybrid of an HMO and a PPO. The insured can chose to either have a general practitioner coordinate their care or opt to go directly to the point of service. The insured has three options for medical care: (a) Through a primary care physician—similar to an HMO plan. Insured just has a co-payment; (b) PPO network provider services the insured can receive services from a PPO provider that is in the network. The insured will have to make a co payment and may also be liable for coinsurance; (c) Services from non-network providers—some of the medical expenses will be reimbursed. It is vital that the insured reads the benefits summary. Make certain you know who pays for what and how much. There is usually a co-payment and a higher coinsurance charge. This is also a deductible. The higher the deductible, the lower the premium payment is.

In general, health insurance plans with higher deductibles have lower premiums to pay. But, the out-of-pocket expenses are much greater. To compensate for the higher out of pocket expenses, the insured can contribute to a health saving account (HSA)—there are tax advantages to doing this. The contributions to the plan can be used to reduce the insured's taxable income. If payments are made by the employer on behalf of an employee, they are tax free. The money in the HSA plan can be used at anytime to pay for approved medical expenses. **Ask your employer about this great plan**.

Of course you can only purchase the type of health insurance that is affordable to you. You need to analyze your personal situation to discern which is the appropriate coverage for you and your family. My recommendation is for you to write down the pros and cons of each health insurance plan you are considering. Next to each plan write down the cost of the plan, deductibles, coinsurance, any other out-of-pocket expenses. Then consider if something catastrophic occurred, ask yourself, "would my family and I be protected with this plan or would it be a financial hardship for us?" Would we be financially devastated? Only you can determine which plan is best for you and your family.

Just remember that for any out-of-pocket expenses you may be confronted with, you may want to begin to amass that money in a separate envelope so that the money is available in time of need. It is always easier taking money from an envelope that has been accumulated, instead of taking it from current income. This is why I spoke earlier about creating an *emergency fund*, it is vital to your financial plan and financial success. If it is very difficult for you to set aside that additional money for medical expenses, the emergency fund is even more critical and vital for you to have established quickly.

As a side note, if you are purchasing health insurance outside of your employer because the employer does not offer it or you are self employed or retired, or whatever the reason, shop around for your coverage. Just don't settle on the first carrier you speak to. It's your hard-earned money; be a good steward of your money. You will be a bit surprised at the difference in premiums. The money you save is extra money for you and your family. Take charge; be assertive and ask questions.

Action Plan

Action Plan

DISABILITY INSURANCE

*D*isability Insurance is used to replace a percentage of the income you as a wage earner earn. I will use the term *disability income* because that's what disability insurance provides, it provides disability income when you become disabled. This kind of insurance protection is extremely important. It cannot and should not be overlooked. It has a significant place in your financial plan. This is one of the reasons for **credit card abuse**. A wage earner becomes disabled and loses his/her income. Without income, the first available source of buying power that the average person thinks about is the **credit card.** So the credit card is used for purchases, but the credit card user is unable to pay the bill when it arrives. The minimum amount on the balance due is not paid because there is no income. Before you know it, the problem exacerbates, and it gets out of control. Don't allow this happen to you, yes you! You will destroy your credit rating and place yourself in a deeper hole.

Most people want to protect their valuable assets: home, personal belonging, car, and so forth, and they want to accumulate money for the future. But many of these same people don't protect themselves against the financial threat of a disabling illness or injury. No financial plan is complete and protected without adequate disability protection. No one, unless you are very opulent, will be able to survive a disability without wiping out all of their savings. Even if you saved 5 percent of your annual income per year, a one -year total disability could wipe out 20 years of savings. Would a bank loan money to someone with no source of income? Can a working spouse, be a spouse, parent, private nurse, and primary wage earner at the same time—and for how long? If you are forced to liquidate your assets for immediate money, what will the fair market value be in a forced liquidation? Six out of ten people who apply for social security benefits never collect them. Yes, sixty percent will never receive a disability social security check. That's why they have lawyers who just specialize in that field. Do not place yourself and your family in this terrible situation.

These are some hard questions and an unconformable position to be in. The good news, there is a better way. The prudent way is disability income. For pennies on the dollar you can protect your income against a disability arising from a injury or sickness, protecting all of your assets, savings and investments from being lost due to a disability.

If your employer offers disability insurance at work **take it**. It will only cost you pennies on the dollar. There are two kinds of disability insurance: short term disability—lasting up to 12 months of disability and long term disability lasting up to age 65. Usually the employer offers the short term with no expense to you. That's why short-term disability kicks in first before the long-term disability kicks in. **Do not pass this coverage up at work.** With all disability programs there is a waiting period. The waiting period could be 30 days, 60 days, 90 days, or 180 days. The shorter the waiting period, the more costly the premium. The longer the waiting period, the lower the premium. Some companies call a waiting period an elimination period. They are the same. It is important to select the proper waiting period for your circumstances. If you have the resources, you can go with a longer waiting period. I would suggest not to have more than a 90-day waiting period. You can run through money very quickly, so make certain you analyze your financial situation carefully.

If your employer does not offer disability insurance and you have to go on your own to purchase it, there are many reputable carriers that offer good coverage. But, you need to put on your Sherlock Homes hat and do some investigating. Here is the scoop in a nutshell. Your premium is determined by your occupation, age, how long you want to be protected; for example (2 years, 5 years, up to age 65), your waiting period; example (30 days, 60 days, 90 days, 180 days, 365 days), and if you add any optional benefits; example (waiver of premium, cost of living adjustment, accidental death and dismemberment) the cost is higher. Depending on the program and company will dictate what benefits are offered.

The better programs will offer 50 percent to 60 percent of replacement of your income due to disability. Usually, if you pay for your disability benefits they should be nontaxable. Make certain you read your policy and understand your benefits. It will also tell you if your benefits are taxable or not. As with all-important documents, keep them stored in a safe place.

If there are two wage earners in the home, both individuals need to have their own disability insurance. No one knows when they will become disabled or who the disabled party will be. Just image what your life would be like with no income. It would be very hard on you and your family. Eliminate the uncertainty of a lost of income and make certain disability income is part of your financial plan.

Action Plan

Action Plan

_____
_____
_____
_____
_____
_____
_____
_____
_____
_____
_____
_____
_____
_____
_____
_____
_____
_____
_____
_____
_____
_____
_____
_____
_____
_____
_____
_____
_____

HOMEOWNER'S INSURANCE

Most people do not plan the insurance for their home; they simply purchase coverage not knowing if they have enough coverage of if they have the proper coverage for their homes. They also don't take into account their deductible on their homeowner's insurance. You could be wasting your hard-earned dollars because you do not have the proper coverage and you have the wrong deductible.

Let's first take a look at when coverage constitute your homeowner's policy:

Coverage A—Dwelling—Covers the house and attached structures for accidental direct physical loss (as provided by your state laws). This includes built in or attached items such as built-in appliances or wall-to-wall carpeting.

Coverage B—Other Structures—Covers other buildings or structures on the property that are separated by a clear space from the house. Examples: detached garage or gazebo, in-ground swimming pool. Amount of coverage is 10 percent of coverage A.

Coverage C—Contents—Covers your personal property, such as furniture and clothing, and items that are not attached to or built into the home (as provided by your policy and state laws). Covers these personal items for loss due to specific causes such as fire, smoke, wind, theft, and other causes as described by the policy. Amount of coverage is determined by your policy. It is usually around 70–75 percent of coverage A. But, check with your policy for the exact amount.

Coverage D—Loss of Use—Pays for reasonable living expenses if you are not able to reside in your home due to a covered loss. (as provided by your policy and state law). Coverage 20% of coverage A.

Courage E—Personal Liability—Covers bodily injury and property damaged to others for which you are held liable. (as provided by your policy and state laws). Covers $100,000, $300,000, $500,000, or other. It depends on what you select. This is a very important coverage because it protects you from lawsuits from others.

Coverage F—Medical Payments to Others—Pays for medical or funeral expenses of others who are injured on your property or by your activities on or off your property. (as provided by your policy and state laws). Coverage is $1,000, $2,000, $5,000, or other. Coverage is whatever you select and the company offers.

You also have a deductible with the policy $500, $1,000, $5,000. This is your choice once you know the available deductibles offered by the company. Deductible minimums vary in each state. Deductible amounts may be raised to reduce premiums and /or make dollars available to purchase essential coverage.

Additional coverage that can be added to the policy are:

- Replacement Cost—Will pay the cost of rebuilding your home at 100 percent. (account for inflation).

- Water Backup or Sewers—Broadens the coverage for loss due to water backup through sewers or drains.
- Scheduled Personal Property—Provides additional coverage for personal property of higher values such as jewelry, watches, furs, and so on.
- Identify Theft—Pays a stated amount for expenses incurred while helping you restore your identity and includes a service to assist you with all tasks to restore your identity. Example $25,000.
- Earthquake—Provided additional coverage for your home, or other structures and personal property due to earthquake damage. A separate deductible applies.

Other types of insurance available for your home:

- Flood Insurance—Coverage for building and contents may be purchased through the National Flood Insurance Program (NFIP). Separate deductible applies to both building and the contents coverage.
- PUL—A Personal Umbrella Policy offers an extra layer of protection for your assets. Coverage is provided for bodily injury, property damage or personal injury to others for which you are held liable. You must maintain certain underlying limits on your auto/homeowner policy to qualify.

Some companies may even offer some other additional coverage and features. I am just exposing you to what is available. This is by no means a mandate that you need all of these options; I am giving you ammunition to be dangerous. You will select coverages that are relevant to your situation.

This coverage is important for every homeowner, because without the essential coverage, you will not be covered against disastrous losses financially. A disastrous loss could wipe out your savings and pile up debts. Once again, here is where the abuse of the credit card evolves. If you cannot pay for your losses, and you need to use a credit card to pay for your loses, what makes you think you can pay the credit card bill in full when it arrives. You can't! If you could, you would not be using a credit card to finance your losses.

Let's say that you have inferior coverage or no coverage at all and your loss is in excess of your coverage. How would you pay for that difference? For example; your house is destroyed by a fire and the coverage A, dwelling coverage, is $150,000, but due to today's market prices, cost of labor and materials, it will cost $250,000 to rebuild your home. Where will you get the shortfall of $100,000? This is reality! The reason for this large discrepancy is because the cost of labor and materials to rebuild your home has increased over the last 10–15 years. But your policy was based on when you first bought the home. This is why all insurance policies have to be *reviewed annually* to adjust for inflation or cost of living.

The same is true if you had guests over to your home and one of those guests hurt themselves in your home. Let's just say that your guest really got hurt, was rushed to the hospital, had a hospital stay, and so forth. Now your guest will lose time from work because of your negligence. One of the steps in your home needed to be repaired and you did not repair it. Now that guest fell due to the broken step and injured his or her spine and is suing you for $150,000, but your homeowner's liability coverage E insures you for $100,000 because that is what you selected at the time you purchased the policy. You are responsible for the additional $50,000. How would you pay for that? I don't know! The injured party could put a lien against your home for the unrecoverable damages or have your paycheck garnished up to 10 percent until the debt is paid for. That's not a good situation to be in. This is why I am providing this information, to protect you from the uncertainties in life. They will happen; we just don't know when. But if you listen, you will be ready and your assets will be well protected.

I recommend that you carry liability coverage in the amount of your financial exposure. Those who have more assets to protect will need to carry more liability coverage. The worst thing that could happen is you build your wealth and you lose some of it or all of it due to a lawsuit. Today people sue for astronomical amounts of money. Be insured, but don't be over-insured. A good way to save money on premiums is to add an umbrella policy. Depending on the company and requirements, you can obtain an umbrella policy which will cover your liability exposure for about $129 per year for a $1 million dollar policy.

You are probably saying to yourself by now, enough with all this insurance. How will I pay for all these coverage? I can't afford it. When I was still in the field I would hear that all the time. "I can't afford it, or I can't afford anymore." My reply was "You can't afford not to afford it." Would you walk across the desert without any water? Would you walk in a blizzard without winter clothes on? Of course not! So why would you leave yourself exposed and unprotected. If you do, you will never be able to accumulate wealth and adhere to a budget plan. If you are having trouble controlling your credit card use, don't worry you will have more credit card use than ever before to cover your losses. Therefore, how do you plan on getting out of debt and being debt-free?

Back to the homeowner's policyholder policy: As far as deductibles go, I select a deductible that I know I will be able to cover with no problem. I used to have a $500 deductible but noticed with my present carrier that I was getting a substantial decrease in premium when I raised the deductible to $2500. The difference in the premium from a $500 to a $2500 deductible was so substantial, that after five years I was able to amass that deductible and place it in an envelope in case I needed to use it. Or I could invest it in a safe liquid investment, but just have it earmarked for my homeowner's insurance. You could do the same.

I see many of my clients carry a $250 or $500 deductible. In my opinion, it is a waste of your hard-earned money. Your premium is so much more costly because of that low deductible. See the insurance companies do not want to waste their time on small claims. It is too expensive for them and unprofitable. So they *reward* you by increasing your deductible and giving you a lower premium payment, because they know that they will not have to deal with frivolous claims.

Only you can make the final decision. Only you will know what is right for you and your family. Don't waste your money on a *low deductible* and don't have the *wrong coverage*. Be *protected*! It's your money and the more you keep in your pocket the better you will be financially, so make certain you protect yourself against uncertain losses by selecting the proper coverage and deductibles.

As I mentioned earlier, *I cannot guaranteed that you will be rich, but if you stay with me, I promise you that you will never be poor.* Keep reading, you will see the total financial plan that you will be building. *You will be out of debt and stay out of debt.* It is easy to show someone how to get out of debt, but the real key is to stay *debt-free*. So keep reading, you are going for a ride. Right now we are still building the foundation to the house.

When you are finished reading this book and put this information into action, your foundation will be rock solid. It will be like the "Rock of Gibraltar." You will be able to withstand those uncertain and unforeseen financial hardships.

116

Action Plan

Action Plan

_____
_____
_____
_____
_____
_____
_____
_____
_____
_____
_____
_____
_____
_____
_____
_____
_____
_____
_____
_____
_____
_____
_____
_____
_____
_____
_____
_____
_____

AUTOMOBILE INSURANCE

*A*utomobile insurance is the most overlooked insurance protection that people don't think about carefully. When I was visiting with some of my clients in October of 2011, I was astonished to see how many of them had just the minimum amount of auto insurance protection that was required by their state. They had left themselves open to a potential lawsuit. Ponder this as you drive each and every day: do you see an inundated amount of automobiles on the road? Of course you do! With all those people driving and usually in a hurry there is bound to be an accident. And I am certain that you see plenty of accidents on the road. My point is, it is just a matter of time before you or someone you know is in an auto accident, your auto is vandalized, or it is stolen.

At times when there is an accident someone is taken away in an ambulance. Automobiles are being towed away. Without the proper protection, who will pay for the auto repair, replacement of the auto if it is totaled, the person being taken to the hospital in an ambulance? If you are at fault or not at fault those bills could be yours to pay. A loss could wipe out your entire savings account without the proper coverage.

Let's take a close look at the components of an automobile policy and its coverage.

- Liability—Coverage for bodily injury and property damage.

- Bodily Injury—Covers damage resulting in bodily injury or death sustained by others, including covered medical costs, which you become legally responsible for as a result of a covered accident. This coverage also provides for your legal defense if a lawsuit is brought against you as a result of a covered accident, including your reasonable out-of-pocket expenses, which you may incur at the insurance company's request.
- Property Damage—Covers damage to another person's property or vehicle that you are legally responsible for as a result of a covered accident. This coverage also provides for your legal defense if a lawsuit is brought against you as a result of a covered accident.

An example of how liability coverage is written is as follows: $100,000/$300,000/$100,000. The first number, $100,000, represents *bodily per person,* the second number, $300,000, represents *per accident,* and the third number, $100,000, represents *property damage.* So what does this mean? It means that if you were in an accident involving two people in the other car, they were injured, and their car was damaged by you, your insurance would pay up to $100,000 per person and up to $300,000 for the entire accident. The damage to the auto would pay up to $100,000. So if the two people injured sued you for $150,000 each, the insurance company would only pay them up to $100,000 each. If four people were injured in the auto accident, the insurance company would pay up to $300,000 for the four injured people. The settled amount would be determined by how much each party is suing for, but the total payout for that accident would be $300,000. Anything above that amount you would be responsible for.

Case in point: let's say you are driving down the road, and at the stoplight you made a left turn and ran into a

BMW. Let's say that you totaled the 740i and injured the driver. The reason why you hit the BMW was because you were texting and didn't notice that the traffic light was red when you decided to make your left turn. The BMW is totaled, and the driver has to be air lifted to a hospital. The replacement of the BMW is $85,000, the driver's hospital expenses are $30,000, and you are being sued for $50,000 due to loss of work to the injured party. Your coverage is $25,000/$50,000/$10,000.

I don't know how to say this to you, but unless you have a lot of money in your bank account, you had better run for the hills. Here is the scoop in nutshell. Your bodily injury will only pay $25,000 toward the payment of hospital expenses of $30,000 and the $50,000 you are being sued for is out of your pocket because your $25,000 of bodily injury has just been used up. The cost to replace the BMW is $85,000; your coverage is $10,000. You are responsible for the $75,000 difference. As you can see you are in deep, deep water. You will have to pay out of your pocket a total of $130,000. ($5,000 (left over hospital expenses) + $50,000 (amount being sued for it awarded)+ $75,000(left over expenses to replace BMW) = $130,000.

This example is reality! No one sues for thousands of dollars anymore. They sue for hundreds of thousands and at times millions of dollars. Remember the story a few years back about the woman who sued McDonald's for millions of dollars because she dropped hot coffee on her lap. McDonald's paid! Don't be under insured with your automobile. In this example it could cost you 20 years or more of your hard-earned money that you saved. Please don't be foolish. Your future and your budget would be devastated.

Other Parts of the Automobile policy:

- Comprehensive—Covers damage to your vehicle not caused by a collision or upset. Examples include damage or loss resulting from contact with animals, theft, vandalism, and glass breakage along with other non-collision related accidents. (subject to deductible) Examples of deductibles are $100, $250, $500, $750, $1,000, and $1,500. Remember the lower the deductible, the higher the premium. I like to have $500 to $1,000 deductible, depending which auto I am insuring. Don't be foolish and carry any deductible under $500. It is a waste of money.

- Collision—Covers damage to your vehicle resulting from collision with another vehicle or object. (subject to deductibles) Examples of deductibles are $100, $250, $500, $750, $1,000 and $1,500. Again I recommend nothing lower than $500. Over time when the vehicle has depreciated to a point where collision does not make sense, you can drop the collision coverage and save money.

I want you to be insured, not insurance poor. I want you to be protected and your assets protected. I do not want you to be indiscreet with your money. We need that discretionary income for investing and savings. But, we cannot build our portfolio until you have the proper coverage and protection. Remember, a catastrophic or disasters could wipe out you portfolio instantly. Just as I mentioned earlier you cannot build a house on sand. You need a solid foundation; that is what I am showing and explaining to you, a solid foundation. Once the solid foundation is established, you will be able to sleep at night like a baby knowing that you are protected against the financial uncertainties of life. I am giving you the meat and potatoes. It is not as overwhelming as it may appear. I am giving you a lot of schemata because I do not want anyone to take advantage of you. After you digest this and regurgitate this wealth of information you will feel good.

Other parts of the automobile policy:

- Supplementary Uninsured/Underinsured Motorists—Covers damage due to bodily injury, including covered medical costs, resulting from a covered accident that you and others are legally entitled to receive from a driver who is not insured or whose insurance limits are not enough to reimburse you for damages they caused. Bodily Injury examples: $25,000/$50,000, $50,000/$100,000, $100,000/$300,00 etc. See what your insurance carrier offers. This is good additional coverage that is inexpensive.
- Personal Injury Protection (PIP)—Eligible injured parties, including passengers and pedestrians are entitled to benefits for a portion of their verifiable wage loss, medical expenses and essential services incurred as a result of a covered accident. This additional protection is inexpensive.

Your insurance carrier may offer other types of coverage, bells and whistles. I have given you what I feel are important coverage for you to understand and choose from. Don't forget, you shop around for your automobile insurance coverage. You will be surprised how much money you can save by shopping around.

The main thing with an insurance company is to make certain they have a good, A+ rating. You can check their rating with A.M. Best Company. Rating is important; you want to make certain the insurance carrier can pay their claims. Many of the well-known companies will have good rates because they are fighting for your business. Do not go with a fly-by-night company. Do your homework and procure the proper coverage for yourself and your family at the right cost.

Action Plan

_____
_____
_____
_____
_____
_____
_____
_____
_____
_____
_____
_____
_____
_____
_____
_____
_____
_____
_____
_____
_____
_____
_____
_____
_____
_____
_____
_____
_____
_____

Action Plan

_____

_____

_____

_____

_____

_____

_____

_____

_____

_____

_____

_____

_____

_____

_____

_____

_____

_____

_____

_____

_____

_____

_____

_____

_____

_____

_____

_____

_____

INVESTING

*I*nvesting—committing a certain amount of money into a vehicle that will yield you a profit or gain. The purpose of investing is to procure a return that will increase your initial investment amount of principle invested. *Only two things earn money: people earn money and money earns money.* The concept of investing is to have your money work for you. The only way to have your money work for you is, after you tithe, to pay yourself first. You must pay yourself first before you pay any of your bills. The majority of people pay their bills first, and when it comes to paying themselves there is very little left over or no money at all left for investing. Where does that leave them? It leaves them with no money or very little.

Only careful financial planning can allow you to have a future that is certain. If you do not prepare for the future, you will have a bleak future that will be uncertain. It bears repeating, people don't plan to fail ... they fail to plan! You must realize that paying yourself first before you pay your bills is the only way for you to move forward and start to amass not only wealth, but also financial freedom. Wouldn't it be nice to not have to worry about money? Of course! Ask yourself "why do I work?" You work to earn money. You earn money to live, take care of your biological needs, and hopefully to be able to doing something for yourself as a reward. But what will happen if you do not save/invest for your future, and you cannot go to work anymore because your body just does not allow you to. That is a fact that is inevitable. It happens to all of us. There comes a time where the human working machine just breaks down where you cannot work anymore—or you have to work less. I am not speaking about disability. I am alluding to the fact that you just cannot get up to go to work anymore. You have had it! You are done mentally and physically.

You need to start to think about the importance of savings/investing for your future. You need to put money aside (save) and invest that money to get a return on your money so it grows. If you continue with your same habits and spend everything you earn, you will never be able to save/invest for your future. That will be a very sad day.

There are those of us who say, "I am still young, I can wait," or "I have no money to save/invest, saving/ investing is only for the rich." First of all you are never too young to start to save/invest. The beauty of starting to invest at such a young age is that the years you have to allow your money to multiply. You need the proper investments and years to have your money increase, grow, multiple. Do you know that with the proper investments and the proper number of years you have till retirement, if you start early, you will amass wealth beyond your imagination. Case in point: let's say you are 23 years old and are able to save just $1,200 per year. You save your money until retirement, which according to current laws will be age 67. If you just saved $1,200 once per year and your average rate of return was 8 percent for the next 44 years, you would accumulate $428,339.57 in today's dollars. Oh that's not a lot of money. What about inflation? My money will be worth nothing. Okay, excuse after excuse.

Think about this, if you don't heed to my advice and you **do nothing**, you won't have to be concerned about $428,339.56 not being a lot of money or it being worthless. You will have a lot less than zero; you will have *nothing.* That's the thinking of a fool. If someone handed you the $428,000 at age 67 would you tell them, "no thank you; keep it. It is not enough," or would you take it? It's okay, I know the answer, you can say it, yes I know, you would take it. Of course you would. If you invested $100 monthly, at the beginning of each month, instead of $1,200 at the end of the year, your investment would be worth $489,120.30. The difference is due to compounding interest. Instead of investing once per year, it is wiser to invest systematically at the beginning of each month. Just for fun, if the same $1,200 was invested annually at 10 percent, this is your new figure; $861,485.80, if invested at the beginning of the month at $100 per month, your investment would be worth $955,649.60. Almost one million dollars. The choice is yours; you can wait and *procrastinate* or get on the train because it is pulling out of the station.

Look at it this way, the train pulls into the station, and the conductor announces to all of the passengers that the train is serving steak and lobster. The train will be pulling out of the station in two minutes, and you just don't like steak and lobster, you love it! The conductor makes the final call and states, this is a special train and it may not be back again. As the conductor makes the final call and blows the whistle, what are you going to do? Are you going to remain on the platform or get on the train? If you want to eat, you will get on the train. It is the same philosophy when it comes to investing. The early bird catches the worm. Starting early is imperative. We will discuss the cost of procrastination later.

Many people will make the excuse that they have no money to invest; you and I know that is not true. If you have no money, you are not adhering to your budget and are living beyond your means. You must make the adjustments immediately. Sit down right now and go over your budget, cut back and find the discretionary income to invest. No, do it now! Saying you have no money is an excuse, you know it, and I want you to know that I know it, too. Stop spending on wants versus needs. Do you get the picture? As far as your excuse that investing is only for the rich. How do you think they became rich? Do you think they let the train pull out of the station without getting on it? Of course not, they were the first ones on the train. They invest, because they know it is the prudent thing to do. *Stop* all of the *excuses*.

This is your time and the time is *now!!! Invest!*

Why do people save/invest? People save/invest for many, many different reasons. Let's look at several different reasons:

- Business Opportunities
- Home Purchase
- Education
- Retirement
- Vacation
- Second Home
- Investment Opportunities
- Emergencies
- Boat
- Automobile
- Financial Independence
- Charities

These are just some of the reasons why people save and invest their money. Whatever your reasons are, you have to *start now* to get it done. The time is now!

Let's look at some different kinds of investments. Some are more volatile than others. The types of investments you select are based on your risk tolerance, what the investments are for, duration of investments, and so forth. The higher the risk, the greater is the potential for return on your investment. The lower the risk, the less potential return there will be on your investment. It all depends on what you can stomach. Do not be foolish! I recommend to always start out slow so you can learn the ropes of investing. Do not start out being too aggressive. You can lose your entire investment. Remember, there are no guarantees in investing in securities. The *risk* you take depends on you. Do not have someone allure you into assuming more *financial risk* then you can tolerate. It is God's money, entrusted to you. Be mindful of where you invest.

Everyone who invests their hard-earned money or a windfall of money should always be diversified. All prudent investors are well diversified. They do not put all of their eggs in one basket. If you put all of your eggs in one basket and that basket falls, all the eggs will break. And they will! You will have nothing to eat. The same is true with investing. *Diversification* is paramount. Diversification is spreading your investments over different companies and different investment types to maximize your return on investment, which is a means of reducing the risk(s) to which an investment portfolio is exposed. A diversified portfolio does not just invest in bonds or stocks. It will invest in stocks, bonds, cash, or cash equivalents. Your risk tolerance and age will determine your asset allocation percentages.

Places to invest

Your emergency fund has to be kept in a safe investment and readily available. Examples are a savings account, a money market account, or a checking account that pays interest. Whichever one of these savings vehicles you select, keep this money separated from your other money. The *emergency fund* is earmarked for only *emergencies.* Do not commingle with other monies. It is not meant to be invested in anything but a safe investment. It must always be available immediately for any kind of emergency. This fund is not for high return on investment or to be locked or tied up for any period of time.

Bonds are investments where you are loaning money to a company. It creates a debt for that company. Bondholders are the first to be paid if a company becomes insolvent. Bonds are issued by corporations, municipalities, including states, cities, and local governments, the U.S. Government, and federal agencies of the U.S. Government. Bonds are considered fixed-income securities because, at time of purchase, the investor is guaranteed a specific interest rate for the term of the bond. The principal, par value, or face value of a bond is the amount due at maturity. The par value of a corporate bond is usually $1,000. A bond's coupon rate or nominal rate is usually stated as a percentage of the par value to determine the annual interest income. For example a coupon rate of 8 percent would yield $80 per year, which would be paid semi-annually in $40 installments. The maturity date of the bond is when the repayment of the principal is due to the investor.

Be concerned of the bond's rating. Well-known rating services are Standard & Poor's, Moody's, and Dun and Bradstreet. Standard & Poor's bond ratings of AAA through BBB indicate investment quality bonds. BB and B bonds are considered speculative, with uncertainty whether the issuer will be able to meet interest and principal payments. C rated bonds are currently paying no interest. D rated bond by Standard & Poor's indicates that the bond is in default.

Bonds are usually a safe investment, but can be subject to future purchasing power risk due to inflation. Which means that inflation can erode away the future buying power of a bond investment. Bonds do not hedge against inflation. But bonds do have their place. Bonds are a good investment for older people, because they generate a *steady stream of income* through the coupon rate or interest rate. There are also municipal bonds to consider; even though they pay lower interest rates than other bonds, they are exempt from federal taxes, which means that they are often a better deal for investors in high tax brackets. This in especially true for cities like New York City where their residents who buy bonds issued by the city, or funds that buy such bonds; Those bonds are triple tax-exempt: no city, state, or federal tax are due on the interest income. Now that's a beautiful thing. Let's take a closer look.

A tax-exempt bond paying 5 percent interest, for a person in the 28 percent tax bracket is equivalent to 6.94 percent taxable yield. A tax exempt bond paying 5 percent for a person in the 33 percent tax bracket that's equivalent to 7.46 percent taxable yield, which is not bad at all! When you think of bonds, think of *income.*

Let's look at some other bonds:

- Junk Bonds—a high yield bond that has substantial risk attached to it because of the uncertainty of future interest and principal payments. To market these high risk bonds, the issuer has to commit itself to paying a very high interest rate of interest. As an investor desiring to put themselves on the path of financial freedom, I urge you to stay away from these investments. You can earn money in this arena, but you have to be very careful and have a good understanding of this type of investment.
- Series EE Bonds—are sold at 50 percent of its face value, the denomination is $50 to $10,000. They are sold only electronically through Federal Direct. No more paper bonds. When the bond matures you receive the face value of the bond, which should be in about 20 years. Bonds are not transferable. Federal income is deferred until bond is redeemed. If bond is used for qualified

higher education, the qualified taxpayer may be able to exclude some or all of the interest from gross income.

- Series HH Bonds—sold in denominations of $50 to $10,000 for face value. They pay interest semi-annually. The interest is paid for 20 years and is subject to federal taxes, exempted from state/city. Bonds are not transferable.

STOCKS—When you buy a share of stock from a company you become an owner of that company. There are over 8,693 stocks listed in the United States; about 3,796 are listed on the New York State Exchange, 2,788 on the NASDAQ, 749 on the American Stock Exchange, and 1,363 Over-The-Counter. Stocks are a good way to invest, but you have to do your due diligence and investigate the stock you are looking to invest in. Do not invest on hearsay; that's just not a good idea. Whatever company you invest in, you should understand the product(s) the company sells or what the company does to generate revenue. Look at the company's annual report and any other accompanying reports the company may have. Besides looking at the company's financial statements you want to also look at the objectives of the company. Where is the company headed, are they diversified or going to be diversified, do they do business in other countries, and so forth. You want to know where you are investing your money in. Determine if the company's objectives you are about to invest in meet your objectives and needs. You need to do your *research.* Be mindful where you procure your information from, because not all information is accurate.

I personally like to look at companies that usually pay a steady dividend like blue chip companies. Some blue chip companies are McDonalds, Coca Cola, and Exxon just to name a few. There are many more good and solid companies to invest in. Do your homework, research and make certain you invest in companies that meet your goals and objectives. Read the company's prospectus, it has a wealth of information.

Mutual Fund—A mutual fund is a professionally managed investment that pools money from many investors to buy a security. A mutual fund can invest in various industries like beverage, real estate, electronics, metal, technology, and so forth. There are a number of different companies within these different industries. This makes a mutual fund a diversified investment. As with all investments you need to read the prospectus. The mutual fund you invest in depends on your objectives.

Prospectus—A Prospectus contains details on a company's objectives, investment strategies, risks, performance, distribution policy, fees, expenses and management. You can obtain a prospectus from the company's Web site, broker, or company. *Always read the prospectus before you invest.*

Ask questions before you invest. Who is managing the fund? What is the fund manager's background? How long has he or she been managing the fund? What kinds of returns has this fund manager had in the past five or ten years. Has the fund manager recently changed? Why is there a new fund manager? Ask, ask, and keep on asking questions before you invest. *Remember hindsight is 20/20.*

There are basically three investor profiles:

- Conservative Investor—You may be concerned by significant short term ups and downs in your account value and prefer slow, but steady, long-term growth.

- Moderator Investor—You may be able to tolerate some ups and downs in your account value. You may be concerned with the safety of your money, but want investment returns that can outpace inflation.
- Aggressive Investor—You may be able to tolerate significant short-term ups and downs in your account value and want maximum long-term growth.

Now you can determine what type of investor you are. It all depends on your risk tolerance. Do not invest in any security that you cannot tolerate its risk. Every security comes with some type of risk. You have to decide on the amount of risk you want to take and what your objective(s) are in investing in a particular security. *Just note that past performance of a security is no indication of how it will perform in the future.*

There are over 7,600 mutual funds to choose from. You will unequivocally be able to find the fund that is right for you and meets your objective(s). To break it down, let's discuss some of the different kinds of mutual funds.

- Growth Funds—Designed for investors seeking capital appreciation over the long term.
- Growth and Income Funds—Combines growth potential of a stock fund with the income potential of a bond fund.
- Asset Allocation Funds—Your assets are allocated among stocks, bonds and cash.
- Global Funds—Invests in companies in the United States and overseas.
- International Funds—Invests in companies outside the United States.
- Income Funds—Invests in U.S. Government securities that pay regular monthly income.

- Tax-Exempt Funds—Designed for investors seeking tax relief. Pays monthly income eligible for exclusion from federal income taxes.
- Index Fund—Aims to replicate the movement of an index. Much l, S&P 500.
- Exchange Traded Funds—Hold assets in stocks, commodities, bonds, trades close to net asset value over the course of the trading day.
- Money Market Funds—Invests in short term money market instruments.

This will give you a good grasp as to how mutual funds work. Mutual funds are another good investment due to their diversification. You can invest in so many different companies through one mutual fund. Besides reading the prospectus, understand the fund managers concept on how he/she selects the companies they invest in. Your fund is only as good as the manager of the fund and the vision of the companies the manager invests in. A company having a solid balance sheet is important. Companies that have less outstanding liabilities will be more solvent in uncertain economic times.

There are so many other places to invest: Savings Accounts, Certificate of Deposits, Real Estate Investment Trusts, Limited Partnerships, Puts/Calls, Gold, Silver, Collectibles, Futures, Cattle, Oil, Sugar, Wheat Gas, Coal Real Estate, Annuities, etc.

My recommendation is, as you invest, to start out slow and grasp a good understanding of what you want to invest in. Diversification is the key to investing; it minimizes losses and maximizes gains. Once you have established your emergency fund, eliminated consumer debt, and have at least $1,000 cash on hand in your home, you can start to invest. If you start to invest before establishing your emergency fund and that emergency arises you could be forced to sell at an uncomfortable time. What I mean, is your investment may be on a decline due to market and economic conditions, and you may get less then you thought. You could take a *loss!* Make certain you have an emergency fund before you start to invest. *Never borrow to invest.*

The first place you should invest is at work. If your company offers a retirement plan like a 401K grab it. If your company offers a matching percentage like 3- or 4-percent or more, run and grab it. It is free money. After you invest at work you want to buy some mutual funds that meet your objectives. Once you feel comfortable with investing, look at some blue chip company stocks to start off with and start to buy a few shares at a time or place a dollar limit like $1,000 or $2,000 on your investment. Once you feel good about the performance of the stock(s) you can buy more. Eventually you may even buy other stocks that you have researched and meet your objectives. There are plenty of good performing stocks that you can invest in. Remember to *diversify;* it is very important.

If you are looking for just growth, you will hold back from buying bonds. But if you want to receive a steady flow of income, bonds are the way to go. I usually buy bonds when I am seeking income. After you feel very confortable with investing and understand the cycle of investing, you can start to look at oil, gas, and other commodities if you choose to. You do not have to. Just don't start to invest in commodities until you under-stand investing and have already built a solid investment portfolio. Commodities are very volatile and are riskier. Just beware! Remember, do not invest in anything you do not understand.

My objective is to get you to save/invest 30 percent of your income each and every pay period. Here is the scoop! Make 10 percent investments that are liquid, like cash, money market, savings, and the other 20 percent invested in 401K, IRA, stocks, mutual funds, and so forth. You need to have liquidity because you never know when a good investment opportunity, like real estate, land, or a business opportunity, will present itself.

Now you can start to realize how you can become financially secure and independent. This is all a mindset, and you need to recondition yourself and the way you think about money. You can always spend the money, but cannot only save and invest it. If you don't have money, you cannot invest and save. It is that simple. After you tithe, *pay yourself first!!* Now I know money is not everything, but it is sure nice to have some. You need it to live and to survive. *Money gives you options.* Having options is a great place to be in.

For those of you who are very conservative or are reaching retirement age and seek less volatility, I have invested in Certificate of Deposits (CDs) by using a step-up process. I would buy a 6-month, 12-month, 18-month and 24-month CDs. As you can see, a CD will be maturing every 6 months so I will be able to reassess my financial position and determine if I want to continue. It also allows me to get the best rates possible.

Below is a chart that exposes the cost of waiting to invest. *Don't procastinate!!*

Assumed 8% Interest Rate   *Age 35*

YEARS	DEPOSIT	AMOUNT	YEARS	DEPOSIT	AMOUNT
1	2,000.00	2,000.00	1	0	0
2	2,000.00	4,160.00	2	0	0
3	2,000.00	6,492.80	3	0	0
4	2,000.00	9,012.22	4	0	0
5	2,000.00	11,733.20	5	0	0
6	2,000.00	14,671.86	6	0	0
7	2,000.00	17,845.61	7	0	0
8	2,000.00	21,273.26	8	0	0
9	0	22,975.12	9	2,000.00	2,000.00
10	0	24,813.13	10	2,000.00	4,160.00
11	0	26,798.18	11	2,000.00	6,492.80

12	0	28,942.03	12	2,000.00	9,012.22
13	0	31,257.39	13	2,000.00	11,733.20
14	0	33,757.98	14	2,000.00	14,671.86
15	0	36,458.62	15	2,000.00	17,845.61
16	0	39,375.31	16	2,000.00	21,273.26
17	0	42,525.33	17	2,000.00	24,975.12
18	0	45,927.36	18	2,000.00	28,973.13
19	0	49,601.55	19	2,000.00	33,290.98
20	0	53,569.67	20	2,000.00	37,954.26
21	0	57,855.24	21	2,000.00	42,990.60
22	0	62,483.66	22	2,000.00	48,429.85
23	0	67,482.35	23	2,000.00	54,304.24
24	0	72,880.94	24	2,000.00	60,648.58
25	0	78,711.42	25	2,000.00	67,500.47
26	0	85,008.33	26	2,000.00	74,900.51
27	0	91,809.00	27	2,000.00	82,892.55
28	0	99,153.72	28	2,000.00	91,523.95
29	0	107,086.02	29	2,000.00	100,845.87
30	0	115,652.90	30	2,000.00	110,913.54

COST OF WAITING

In the above chart the person to the left contributed $16,000 into saving/investing, while the other person waited eight years, and then started to contribute for the next twenty-two years, totaling $44,000 in contributions. The second person contributed more than two and a half times more money, but has less money after 35 years. Why?, because he waited. It is the same investment principal, the compounding of interest over time. Nothing special, nothing magical, just the right attitude. Imagine if the amounts were larger, the impact would be that much more. Don't wait. It will cost you too much money. It's time to step to the plate. The time to start is *now! Invest!*

One final note: It is more beneficial to invest a steady amount periodically then to invest just a lump sum. *Dollar Cost Averaging* (DCA) lowers the average per share cost of your stock/mutual fund holding by ensuring that you buy more shares when prices are down and fewer shares when they are up. Besides Dollar Cost Averaging, it is also a great idea to *reinvest your dividends* from stocks or mutual funds. By reinvesting your dividends, you will own more shares thereby increasing the value of your holdings. With mutual funds you can also reinvest capital gains to increase the amount of shares you own in that fund. This will also help to increase the value of your portfolio over time.

This is a *cardinal rule* I learned a long time ago, never invest in something you do not understand.

Action Plan

_____

_____

_____

_____

_____

_____

_____

_____

_____

_____

_____

_____

_____

_____

_____

_____

_____

_____

_____

_____

_____

_____

_____

_____

_____

_____

_____

_____

_____

_____

Action Plan

TAXES

*T*axes are inevitable, they are part of life, but you can minimize the taxes that you pay. In the Retirement chapter you will see retirement plans that will help you to reduce your taxable income. Anytime you reduce your taxes, it is a beautiful thing. Some of my clients also invest some of their money in annuities, besides a salary reduction plan like a 401k. An annuity will allow you to defer your tax consequence on your investment until you are ready to surrender the annuity. You will not be able to surrender the annuity until 59.5 years old. If you surrender the annuity before age 59.5 you will have to pay a 10 percent premature penalty and be subject to federal income tax in the year of distribution.

This nonqualified plan will be taxed based on the growth of the annuity. For example; you invest $100,000 into the annuity. At age 65 you surrender the annuity, it has grown to $230,000. You will pay taxes based on the gain of the annuity which is $130,000. ($230,000 – $100,000 = $130,000 gain). At that point of time you could be in a lower tax bracket.

Any investments that you make in stocks, bonds, or mutual funds not placed in a qualified plan like a 401k or IRA will be taxed on the gain of the investment when sold. If you have a gain you will report it on schedule D of the 1040. If you have a loss you will report that as well on schedule D of the 1040. But you will only be able to report losses up to a maximum of $3,000. Any loss over

$3,000 can be carried over into future years until the loss has been absorbed.

When you withdraw your money from the 401k or IRA upon retirement you will be selling your shares to receive the proceeds. At that time you will be responsible for paying income taxes on those investments. Your tax consequences will be based on your tax bracket and the amount of shares sold.

The advantage of the 401k or IRA is that it allows you to save money on a tax-free basis. It will also help you to reduce your tax liability by the amount of your contributions. You will need to know what you are allowed to contribute based on your income and if you have a retirement plan at work for those who want to contribute into an IRA.

Make certain you file your tax returns on time. If you need more time file an extension, it will add six months to when the tax return will be due. So instead of the return being due on April 15, you will have until October 15 to file your tax return. You must still pay whatever tax you owe by April 15. If you do not pay your tax bill by April 15, expect interest and penalties to be added to the amount of tax you owe. My recommendation is to hire a qualified tax preparer to prepare your income taxes if you do not feel qualified. If it is over your head to prepare your tax returns, leave it to the professionals.

As of this writing by *December 31, 2013* every paid tax preparer must pass an exam in order to prepare tax returns. Once the test is passed they will be granted the designation of Registered Tax Return Preparer. The only exceptions are CPAs, Attorneys, and EAs (Enrolled Agents). If the person preparing your return is not one of the individuals I mentioned, that person is prohibited from preparing your tax return for a fee, as of this writing.

An Enrolled Agent is the top in the field of taxation. An individual, who wishes to become an Enrolled Agent, has to pass three difficult exams. All of these exams have to do with taxes only, nothing else but taxes. After that individual passes all three exams, they have to adhere to a background check before he or she is admitted to practice before the IRS. An Enrolled Agent is an expert in the field of taxation.

My recommendation is to keep your tax returns for ten years. The government can go back three years and audit your returns. But if fraud is involved, there is no time frame. Keep good and accurate records, including any item that you have used to generate a tax credit, deductions, adjustments to income or any expenses that you are allowed. You need to keep all of those records in a safe place. Keep detailed records of all your expenses, such as receipts, log books for mileage used for business reasons, spreadsheets, canceled checks, any kind of statements, and so forth. It is wise to use a tax professional so that you receive all the tax deductions, credits, and adjustment you are entitled to. If your tax professional is on the ball he or she can help you prepare for the following tax year and develop a plan of actions to reduce your taxable income. Over the years I have advised many of my clients that there are options available for them to reduce their taxable income. For example: In 2010 I acquired a new client and noticed that she was not making any contribution to her 401K plan. After speaking with her and going over the benefits of a 401K, she decided to contribute 6 percent of her salary into the 401K. In 2011 she reduced her taxable income and received extra refund of $930.00. Her income was $62,000 x 6 percent contribution into the 401K = $3,720 x 25% tax bracket = $930.00 in savings. This is why it is imperative to get the right tax professional for your self. A knowledgeable tax professional can help you to lower your taxable income by showing you how you can gift assets to charitable organizations, what deductions and credits you are entitled to, and to help you plan for the future, so you can have more of your money to utilize instead of the government. Giving to charitable organizations will help you to lower your tax liability, resulting in paying less tax and helping your favorite charity. It's a win-win situation.

For individual taxes Publication 17 is available from the Internal Revenue Service. This Publication will cover everything that is applicable to preparing individual taxes. It will also refer you to other Publications when more of an in depth understanding is needed pertaining to a particular topic. It will address exemptions, standard deductions, taxable income, adjustments to income, allowable credits and deductions, plus a lot more on the subject of taxes.

Any time you call the Internal Revenue Service make note who you are speaking to and ask for their ID number. Keep this information and the topic of discussion with the applicable tax year. You may just need this information for the future. Also, do not be surprise if you receive a different answer on a specific topic from a different Internal Revenue employee. This is why it is important to keep records on your conversations with the Internal Revenue Service.

For you to take advantage of tax shelters for your individual situation I encourage you to consult a financial planning professional or a tax professional like an Enrolled Agent. A qualified professional will be able to assess your situation and readily offer you with suggestions that will help you to reduce your tax liabilities and help you to shelter your money from taxation.

There are just too many variables that come into play for me to just make a list of tax shelter investments that are applicable to your individual situation. The purpose of this chapter is to make you aware that people can protect their investments from taxation. Don't be afraid to seek help from the professionals. This is why there are specialist in the field of taxation. No one can know everything. Do not expect one person to know it all.

Action Plan

Action Plan

RETIREMENT

*R*etirement is a very important aspect to financial freedom. When you are ready to retire you do not want to be confronted with questions, such as, "will I have enough money to retire on, or will I still have to work during my retirement years?" You do not want to put yourself in that precarious situation. It is not where you want to be. But if you have been absorbing, understanding, and are ready to adhere to the suggestions made, you will have nothing to be concerned about. Retirement is a time for you to do what you want to do when you want to do it, no questions asked.

In August of 2012, I acquired a new client who was having a difficult time managing her money. She is a self-employed consultant in Brooklyn, New York. She generates anywhere from $250,000 to $330,000 in gross receipts. After expenses and taxes she nets between $140,000 and $197,000. After speaking with her and establishing a budget for her, it was revealed that she was behind in paying her taxes and only had $5,200 for retirement. Here is the real problem. She is 63 years old. What do you do with a client who owes the government money, has no savings, and only has $5,200 for retirement? Unfortunately, this very fine lady will not be retiring soon. Please don't put yourself in that situation. Just do what is suggested in the book and you will become financially free. As I mentioned in the investment chapter, do not procrastinate. It will not only be costly, it could be deadly to your financial survival.

Let's take a look at some of the retirement vehicles that will help you to achieve your retirement goals and objectives. In the old days there was a program offered by employers called a *defined benefit*. A defined benefit retirement program was offered by the employer, who paid a monthly benefit to the retired employee, based on age, length of employment, and employee salary history. The employee did not contribute into this program. It is all the based on the employer. This type of retirement program is becoming obsolete. It has become too expensive for employers to provide this type of benefit. You may still be able to find a select few employers offering this benefit.

Another type of retirement program is called a *defined contribution*. With a defined contribution plan the employee makes the contributions to the plan and selects how their contributions should be invested. Examples of defined contributions are 401K, 403B, and 457, (salary reduction). The type of industry you work for will determine the type of plan that the employer offers you. Private industries offer a 401k, nonprofits like school offer a 403b, also known as a Tax Sheltered Annuity (TSA), or a Tax Deferred Annuity (TDA), and government agencies offer a 457 plan.

These are some of the retirement plans you should know about and how they work. **(2013 / 2014 tax rules)**

- IRA—contribution up to $5,500 per year, if 50 and over up to $6,500 per year
- Roth IRA—contribution up to $5,500 per year, if 50 and over up to $6,500 per year
- 401k—contribution up to $17,500 per year, if 50 and over up to $23,000 per year
- 403b—contribution up to $17,500 per year, if 50 and over up to $23,000 per year

- 457—contribution up to $17,500 per year, if 50 and over up to $23,000 per year

There are also annuities that can be used as retirement vehicles. Some of the annuities in the market place are fixed, indexed, variable, or an immediate annuity. A *fixed annuity* will grow at a fixed interest rate, like 3 percent or 3.5 percent. A *variable annuity* allows you to invest in mutual funds. An *index annuity* allows you to invest in the market without taking the risk of losing your money. Your investment is based on the performance of the S&P 500 over a stated period of time with a cap. If the S&P loses money, your investment is protected from the loss. If the S&P yields a 10 percent return over that stated period time and your cap is 7 percent, you will earn the 7 percent on your investment. An *immediate annuity* is an annuity that pays out immediately. This type of plan pays you a monthly benefit until your demise.

A contribution to an IRA will adjust your gross income thereby reducing your taxable income by your contribution amount. In the 25 percent tax bracket a $5,000 IRA contribution will save you $1,250 in taxes. The contributions you make to your 401K, 403B, or 457 plans will also reduce your taxable income. In the 25 percent tax bracket, a 401K contribution of $17,500 will save you $4,375 in taxes. That's a lot of wood. Better the money is in your pocket then in the pocket of the government.

There is a 10 percent penalty if you withdraw you retirement money prior to age 59.5. If you do not take your required distribution by 70.5 you will have a penalty of 50 percent, based on the shortfall of your required distribution. *Know this law!!*

If your employer matches a percentage of your contribution, make certain you contribute at least the amount your employer is willing to contribute. It is *free money,* so take advance of it. It is a 100 percent return on your money. It is a beautiful thing to get free money and get a 100 percent return on your money that your employer is matching. Workers who do not take advantage of this gift are missing the boat. Do not be one of those people who miss the boat. It is wrong and a very unwise choice.

There is also a Roth IRA and a Roth 401K. The Roth IRA does not allow you to take a tax deduction, thereby not reducing your taxable income. But your benefit at the end of the rainbow is tax-free. In addition, you do not have to take your distribution by 70.5 with the Roth IRA. The Roth 401K is funded with after tax dollars contributions, and you have to take distributions by age 70.5. The good news is that you can avert that requirement by converting your Roth 401K into a Roth IRA and can continue to contribute to the plan after age 70.5. Before you can take a distribution at age 59.5 you need to have the Roth IRA for at least five years to avoid the 10 percent penalty. The Roth 401K does not reduce your income; your contributions are still part of your income. But distributions from this program are tax free, they will not be included as income.

As a rule of thumb, taxpayers who are in a high tax bracket usually stay with the traditional programs. Taxpayers who are in a lower tax bracket usually favor the Roth IRA and Roth 401K. The decision is yours. The primary objective is that you start one of these programs and stay with it (them) all the way to retirement. Your future is in your hands. If you do not take action, no one else will do it for you. Take charge, take control, and get it done. You are on your way to financial freedom! Yeah!

There is one other item I want to address with you that I feel that you need to be cognizant of: it is your pension from work if you have a deferred benefit plan. Whatever your maximum monthly payment will be, your spouse will have to sign a waiver that will allow you to take 100 percent of your pension. If your spouse does not sign the waiver you will receive a reduced benefit to provide a reduced benefit for your spouse. If your spouse predeceases you, you will still receive the reduced benefit even though she has passed.

This is how a typical pension plan works. For example, you have a pension of $3,000 per month. If your spouse signs the waiver you will receive $3,000 per month. When you die, your wife receives zero, nothing. If you select to leave money to your spouse after you die, the wavier is not signed. Example: Your monthly pension will yield you $3,000 per month, but since you want your spouse to receive an income in case you die, the calculation is as follows: $3,000 x 80% = $2,400 of monthly income you will receive, so that your spouse receives a reduced benefit of $1,200 per month ($2,400 x 50%) upon your death. So to provide your spouse with 50% of your benefit, it will cost you 20% of your benefit. In dollar terms, that's a $600 per month reduction in your pension benefit per month. Here is what you need to know, if your spouse dies before you, you are still stuck with your reduced pension. You will continue to receive $2,400 per month. I just want to make you aware of how it works so you can plan your retirement effectively.

There is another choice to let you know. It is called the pension trap or *pension maximization.* Instead of losing 20 percent of your pension, you can purchase permanent life insurance to replace the income for your spouse. By doing this, if your spouse dies before you, you will still receive 100 percent of your monthly pension. If your wife does predecease you, you can cash surrender the policy for its value. Now you will receive cash back and still be receiving 100 percent of your pension, ($3,000). It is your pension so be informed so you can make more *intelligent decisions* about your *money.*

Action Plan

Action Plan

_____

_____

_____

_____

_____

_____

_____

_____

_____

_____

_____

_____

_____

_____

_____

_____

_____

_____

_____

_____

_____

_____

_____

_____

_____

_____

_____

_____

_____

_____

_____

_____

Your Estate

*E*state planning is not just for the wealthy; it is for everyone. It involves more than just disposing of one's property. The process encompasses planning for the client's lifetime financial affairs to accumulate, and to preserve assets for eventual disposition at death. When you think about estate planning you think about avoiding estate taxes, but there are other areas that must be considered; providing for loved ones, avoiding family squabbles, or even taking care of the family pet. Let's look at estate planning as the accumulation, conservation, and distribution of assets to achieve effectively a client's objectives while taking into account applicable tax laws.

Estate planning is necessary for planning for minor children and for dependents who are mentally or physically disabled, emotionally disturbed, physically handicapped, or who are unable to handle their personal and business finances. It is also necessary for leaving your assets to certain individuals, institutions, or charities. The importance of estate planning is also important because of all the hard work and effort you have put into getting your financial house in order.

Let's get that financial house in order. The following documents will need to be reviewed to ascertain the objectives that the client has.

- Any current wills

- Any deeds to real estate and mortgage balances
- Financial statements, profit and loss statements, balance sheets
- Income tax returns for the past three years
- Life, health, disability insurance policies, employee benefits—pension
- Property and liability insurance
- Any other relevant documents—trusts, pre-nuptial agreements, divorce decrees, etc.

It is imperative to review and examine these documents periodically. I recommend you reviewing your documents annually. We are in a very fast-paced world, and you want to make certain that those changes are updated. By reviewing your documents you be able to ascertain that your objectives are on target. Yes, it takes time to review and monitor your objectives periodically, but it is well worth it. You may have to update your beneficiaries or will. Let your beneficiaries know which documents they are on. For example you don't want to have a beneficiary on your life insurance policy who is deceased. If you are married, do not leave your spouse in the dark. Include your spouse in your financial decisions and in your annual review of your assets and applicable documents. Everyone needs an exist plan for their assets.

What is probate and how does work? Probate is the court supervised process of distributing your assets as you have outlined in your will or according to the laws of your state of legal residence if you do not have a will. Assets properly titled or with designated beneficiaries can bypass the probate process. Probate fees can be expensive and time consuming. A *will* is important to have because it tells how you want your assets to be distributed and to who. It is the last time your wishes will be carried out.

Besides a will there may be other documents that may be important to you and should be included in your estate plan.

- ***Guardianship***—If you have minor children you want to have a plan that someone you trust will raise your children the way you would raise them in case of your premature death. Without guardianship and a will, you will leave it up to the court to decide for you. The court may not choose who you want. Don't be unprotected in this area of planning; they are your children. Do the right thing for them. My suggestion is to attach a life insurance policy to the guardianship to have the required funds available for your child/children. I know the guardian you choose will show love toward your child. But you cannot expect them to pay for all of your child's needs including education. My suggestion is to leave that insurance policy in a trust for your child with your explicit instructions of how you want the proceeds to be distributed to your child. There are many different types of trusts and you should consult an estate lawyer who is cognizant of these trusts. I suggest you interview three to four estate lawyers to determine which fits your needs and budget best.

- A ***trust*** is a transfer of property to one party for the benefit of the other. The trust must be administrated according to the directions contained in a will, trust agreement or other trust document. In this case to have funds for your children in case of your premature death, this trust will be what we call a funded trust. The trust will avoid probate.

- ***Life insurance*** is a great tool to use for estate planning. One of the beautiful features of life insurance is that it passes to the named beneficiary outside of probate. Another great feature of life insurance is the *spend thrift clause* which will generally protect the beneficiaries from their creditors.

When you are searching for any financial professional to help you, always ask for **references** and always ask them *why!* In addition, ask the financial profession some questions that you already know the answers to so you can determine their integrity and their knowledge of the subject matter. I have no problem with a financial professional telling me that "I am not certain of that subject matter; let me research it and get back to you." I like honesty. What I detest, is when a financial professional or any professional for that matter tries to impress me with some nonsense and just rambles on with just rhetoric. This is your financial plan; you control it and take charge of it. Make certain you feel comfortable with who you are working with.

As of this writing the limit for Federal Estate Taxation for 2013 is $5,250,000, then you are taxed at 40 percent on the excess.

Example: 1
Death 2013
Value of Gross Estate $7,000,000
                      −500,000   allowable debts,
                      _____ expenses, deductions
                      $6,500,000 Gross Taxable Estate

                      $5,250,000 Exemption
                      $1,250,000 Net Taxable Estate
                      x 40%
                      $500,000   Estate Tax Due

Example: 2
Death 2013
Value of Gross Estate $10,000,000
                      − 500,000 allowable debts,
                      _____expenses, deductions
                      $9,500,000 Gross Taxable Estate
                      − $5,250,000 Exemption
                      $4,250,000 Net Taxable Estate

x 40%
<u>*$1,700,000*</u> Estate Tax Due

Don't allow these numbers to alarm you. In today's times it is not difficult to amass millions of dollars in cash, real estate, securities, investments etc. that will be included in your gross estate. I want you to be cognizant that with just an exemption of $5,250,000 in 2013, there will be many taxpayers who will be confronted with an estate tax problem. What do you do? You need to prepare for it. You need to seek help from an expert. Just like you have a doctor when you get sick or need an operation you also need advisers. A stitch in time saves nine. A timely effort will prevent more work later. For estate planning you need to consultant an estate attorney. An estate attorney can help you with trusts, wills, guardianship, and any estate planning related items. But for the **funding** of a trust or procuring **life insurance** to defray the expenses and taxes on the estate, I would suggest an insurance professional. I personally do not like to mix up different services that professionals offer. I want them to also have my best interest at heart not their wallet. I want them to be a master at one trade not a jack of all trades.

In 2014 or any other year, if the Federal Estate Tax exemption changes, you can follow the steps to calculate your estate tax. The point I am driving home is the same. Even though the figures may change you still need to be aware of tax consequences.

Estate taxes are paid by the following means:

1. An ideal situation is to have enough cash in the bank or enough assets that can be converted into cash quickly to pay the estate tax bill.
2. Use life insurance proceeds to defray you estate tax bill.

3. Sell illiquid assets through fire sales or borrow against illiquid assets.

The most pragmatic way to defray estate taxes is by the use of life insurance, not by reducing your estate to pay for the estate taxes. Transfer the *risk* for pennies on the dollar. A good estate attorney can help you minimize your estate tax liability by the use of various estate planning tools. It is smart, it is wise, it is prudent to conserve your estate from the estate taxes. You have worked hard, you have heeded to the advice given in this book, and now you have to complete the mission. You have come so far and have achieved so much. You just have to go a little further. You can do it and make it to the finish line. *I know you can do it!*

If you are opulent you can self-insure, but why would you when you can transfer the risk to an insurance company for pennies on the dollar. If you self-insure, you will pay dollar for dollar, not pennies on the dollar. Many very opulent families like the "Rockerfellers" used life insurance to take care of their risk. The life insurance was in place to pay for the estate taxes. Why not you? Remember, you do not want to be penny wise and dollar foolish.

Another element you should know about in the estate planning area is the annual gift tax exclusion. For 2013 and 2014 the annual exclusion is up to $14,00 to any individual. A husband and wife can give as much as $28,000 to an individual without reducing their lifetime gift exemption of $5,250,000 per person for 2013. The beautiful thing is that a person can give these annual gifts of $14,000 without reducing their lifetime credit also known as the unified credit.

The Unlimited Marital Deduction allows you to pass your entire estate to your spouse free from federal estate taxes. It virtually eliminates these taxes at the death of the first spouse. Many states allow a deduction for a bequest to a surviving spouse. There is a big catch, however. The Unlimited Marital Deduction merely *postpones* the tax until the death of the second spouse. At that time your heirs will be faced with a whopping tax bill unless a proper strategy is put into place

There is an estate-planning tool called **Living Trust with O-Tip and Bypass Trust**. This trust takes into account the Federal Estate Tax Exemption and the Unlimited Marital Deduction. If properly structured, the assets listed will not be included in the surviving spouse's estate. Consultant an estate planning attorney to learn more about this estate planning tool and how to execute it.

Remember you have worked hard all those years; it is up to you to have the proper estate plan established. You want to know what your completed picture will look like. Do you want to cover your debts if you die, ensure a comfortable lifestyle for your surviving heirs, appoint a guardian for your children or set aside funds for future education, divide your estate among your heirs in a certain way, provide for future care of handicapped relative, leave money to charity, or pass a on family business? Estate planning assures that, whatever your goals, your assets are distributed in *your* best interest, not the government's.

Here are some documents you want to be familiar with when you are living, so that when you die, your estate is handled according to your wishes. (Living versus Death)

Living Will—A personalized set of instructions that a person gives that specify what actions should be taken for their health if they are no longer able to make decisions due to illness or incapacity.

Power of Attorney or Health Care Proxy—Where someone is appointed by the individual to make decisions on their behalf when they are incapacitated.

Will—Basic building block of an estate plan. It is a legal document prepared by an attorney, which spells out how you want your property distributed and guardianship for minor children.

Executor/Executrix—A person who is responsible for managing the assets of the estate and for handling the property's ultimate distribution.

Trust—Relationship whereby property is held by one party for the benefit of another.

Intestate—A person who dies without leaving a valid will. State laws then determine who inherits the property.

Administrator—A court-appointed person who represents the estate when there is no will or if an executor/executrix is not named.

Recap of your Estate Plan

- *Determine your objectives*
- *Determine your net worth*
- *Set up a will and / trust*
- *Select an executor/executrix*
- *Shelter your assets from taxes*
- *Review and update your strategy annually*

There is another item concerning estate taxes that you must be cognizant of. In addition to the federal estate tax, there is also a *state* estate tax. Inquire if your state has an estate tax and what the exemption is. It's a good idea to discuss strategies with an attorney who is familiar with your state laws.

Action Plan

_____
_____
_____
_____
_____
_____
_____
_____
_____
_____
_____
_____
_____
_____
_____
_____
_____
_____
_____
_____
_____
_____
_____
_____
_____
_____
_____
_____
_____
_____
_____
_____
_____
_____
_____

Action Plan

_____
_____
_____
_____
_____
_____
_____
_____
_____
_____
_____
_____
_____
_____
_____
_____
_____
_____
_____
_____
_____
_____
_____
_____
_____
_____
_____
_____
_____

Mortgages

*I*was not going to add this to the book, but after pondering it assiduously, I realized there was value and benefits for people who are looking to purchase a home or refinance due to the extremely low interest rates.

It is a great idea to be a homeowner and say that you own your own home. Or you own your own home and want investment property. I have coached many of my clients in investing in real estate and they have done extremely well for themselves. As I coached them, I will ask you some of the questions that I asked them. What is the purpose of owning real estate? Who is it for? Where do you want to purchase the real estate? Why do you want to invest in real estate? When are you looking to invest in real estate? How will you purchase the real estate? The reason why I ask these questions is because real estate is not for everyone. It is a major investment. It will absorb your time and energy. It will take money to maintain the real estate. I want my clients to understand the ramifications of real estate. I request that my client list the pros and cons of owning real estate. If they feel after answering the questions and examining the pro and cons they want to move forward, we will devise a plan of action to help them get there.

Let's discuss some of the facts: No matter what program you select you need down payment money and closing cost money. You also need to maintain your emergency fund. *Do not use your emergency fund for a down payment.* An emergency fund is only for emergencies not for buying things. If you do not put down at least 20 percent of the purchase price you will have to buy private mortgage insurance (PMI), which protects the lender against loss in case of default. Once your loan to value (LTV) equals 80 percent, you can request that the lender eliminate that payment. By law a lender must automatically remove PMI when your LTV reaches 78 percent.

There are different kinds of mortgages: Conventional, FHA, Jumbo, USDA/RURAL, and VA. There may be variations to these programs. There are terms from 10 years to 30 years and in between. The shorter the term, the more of your payment goes towards the principal and less towards the interest. The longer the term, more of your money in the early years goes towards the interest instead of the principal. You do not have to take a 30 year mortgage. My recommendation is to take the mortgage that is comfortable for you. Make certain you can afford the payment. Do not get over your head. If you can afford a 10-year or 15-year mortgage, by all means go for it. You will achieve owning your home earlier and being debt-free sooner. That is what it is all about. It is about being *debt-free.* You want to eventually have no debt and be debt-free always.

In addition, you have the option to apply more money towards the principal of the loan, thereby reducing the number of years remaining on the life of the mortgage. You will pay off the note earlier and save additional money by doing this. Case in point. On the first home that I owned, once I learned and understood that the loan did not have a pre-payment penalty, I paid off a 30 year note in 12 years. This saved me a ton of money. I used tax refund checks, and applied extra money toward the principal every month. After 12 years I was completely debt free.

Remember this is an option that you can control. You do not need to refinance. You do not have to complete any addition paperwork. As long as there is no prepayment penalty, you don't even need permission from the bank. You can apply as much or as little as you choose to payoff your mortgage loan earlier.

Please do not do what I have seen some of my new clients do. They use the equity in their home as a cash machine. For example: let's remodel the home, they refinance; let's go on a vacation, they refinance; let's buy a car, they refinance; let's pay off our credit card debt, they refinance; they keep refinancing. Then they use their credit cards all over again and create more credit card debt. Their immediate answer to their problem is to refinance. They are always refinancing, that they never get to own their home and be debt-free. *Do not use your home as a cash machine. You will head down the path of disaster. Heed my words.* Your home is a safe haven for you and your family. It is not a bank.

As far as refinancing goes, as of this writing, interest rates are at an historical low. For those of you with high interest rates and long terms, I can understand that you want to refinance. I know I am going to sound contradictory, yes the interest rate is important, but more important than the rate is the program. What will the program achieve for you? The way you save the most amount of money is by reducing your term. When refinancing you should consider (1) lowering your monthly payment; (2) cash out if you need to pay off your credit card debt; (3) reduce your term; (4) check to see the tax benefit (deductions on tax return); and (5) see if there is an allowable payment holiday (skipping a payment for 30–60days). You must place yourself in *a stronger and better financial position.* If you are not doing this, why are you refinancing?

Note: Your credit score plays a major role in the program that you will be offered. A credit score of 720 or better is good. The higher your credit score the more options you will have. It is recommended to check you score annually. If you notice something incorrect on the report, do not hesitate to dispute it.

Action Plan

_____
_____
_____
_____
_____
_____
_____
_____
_____
_____
_____
_____
_____
_____
_____
_____
_____
_____
_____
_____
_____
_____
_____
_____
_____
_____
_____
_____
_____
_____
_____
_____
_____
_____

Action Plan

_____
_____
_____
_____
_____
_____
_____
_____
_____
_____
_____
_____
_____
_____
_____
_____
_____
_____
_____
_____
_____
_____
_____
_____
_____
_____
_____

SOCIAL SECURITY

*H*ere are some of the facts you should know about Social Security. I do not know what will happen with Social Security. But as of this writing here is the scoop:

Social Security Benefits

Disability—40 credits needed, 20 of which were earned in the last 10 years ending with the year you became disabled.

Retirement—40 quarters needed to be eligible.

Widower Benefit—can receive benefits as early as age 60—reduced benefit.

Burial—$255 from social security to bury your spouse.

When a breadwinner dies and there are unmarried children involved, the children will receive a benefit until under age 18 or up to age 19 if attending elementary or secondary school full time. If the child has been disabled before the age of 22 the benefits will continue. The widow or widower will receive a benefit until the youngest child attains age 16. The widower's benefit will stop when the youngest child reaches age 16. This is called the *blackout period*. If you are 36 years old when your youngest child attains the age of 16, you will not receive a benefit for

24 years. That is a long time. You will be able to apply for benefits at age 60, but at a reduced benefit. The only exception to this rule is if your child is mentally disabled and you exercise parental control over that disabled child, you may be entitled to benefits. The only way to avert this horrible situation is to have a lot of money, a great job, combination of both, or life insurance in place. The prudent decision is life insurance. A life insurance policy where you are the named beneficiary so you will not have to pay any taxes on the life insurance proceeds. It will not only provide the lost wages it will give you *peace of mind.*

FULL RETIREMENT BENEFITS

1943–1954	age 66
1955	age 66–2mos
1956	age 66–4mos
1957	age 66–6mos
1958	age 66–8mos
1959	age 66–10mos
1960 and later	age 67

You can receive early retirement at age 62 with a reduced benefit if your retirement age is 66. Your benefit will be reduced to 75 percent of your full benefit. A monthly benefit of $1,000 will be reduced to $750 per month at age 62. If you delay your retirement until age 70 you will receive an increased benefit.

Taxation of Social Security Benefits:

	S, HH, QW	MFJ	Taxable S/S
Above	$34,000 +	44,000+	85% MAX
Between	$25,000-$34,000	$32,000-$44,000	50% MAX
Below	0-$25,000	0-$32,000	NONE

Footnote: S= single, HH= head of household, QW= qualifying widow, MFJ= married filing jointly.

For more information contact your Social Security Office or look them up on line. 1–800–772–1213. WWW, socialsecurity.gov

Action Plan

Action Plan

_____
_____
_____
_____
_____
_____
_____
_____
_____
_____
_____
_____
_____
_____
_____
_____
_____
_____
_____
_____
_____
_____
_____
_____
_____
_____
_____
_____
_____
_____
_____
_____

Financial Road to Freedom and Independence

———— ⌐⁄⁄⌐ ————

Now you have arrived at the road to financial freedom and independence. You have to extol yourself for completing this book. Now you must put all of the information you have acquired into action. There are no more tomorrows. Tomorrow is now, and now is the time to just do it. I know it won't be easy. I know it will take time and effort. But the time and effort will be worth it. If it were that easy, everyone would be doing it. It is not easy. It will take time and dedication. Anything worth anything takes time and effort.

Here is the good news. In your hands is the book "Waking up debt-free". This book will help to free you from the enslavement of debt. The only thing holding you back from financial freedom and independence is yourself. Set the time aside to accomplish what will change your financial life forever. You will happy that you did.

The Road to Financial Freedom and Independence

Create your budget: First, list in a book all of your expenses for the next 30 days. I mean everything you spend money on. No matter how little, list it. You must to do this to create a budget that will be accurate. You will obtain a bird's-eye view of what you are spending money on and realize which items are nonsense. These items must be eliminated immediately. Remember needs versus wants.

Emergency fund: Save at least 10 percent of your income until 6–12 months has been accumulated for an emergency. Also, have $1,000 in cash on hand at all times at home.

Which credit card bills do you pay off first? You must make a list of each bill with its respective balance and prevailing interest rate and pay those bills down, one bill at a time.

Saving for something special: Use the envelope system for this.

Insurance planning: *Vital to your future and your success. Need to build that solid foundation.* **See below!**

Life Insurance: Analyze your situation and choose the appropriate type of insurance for your specific needs. Term insurance versus permanent insurance. Life insurance replaces income for your loved ones. Don't leave your family unprotected.

Health insurance: Select the appropriate coverage and deductible to fit your needs and budget. A catastrophic event can wipe out years of saving without the proper protection.

Disability insurance: Check to see what your employer offers. If you need to, buy disability income on your own. If you became disabled, it will replace your income up to 60 percent.

Homeowner's insurance: Make certain you are not over-insured or underinsured.

Check your deductible to make certain it is not too low.

Automobile insurance: The proper protection can avoid substantial money out of your pocket in case of a law suit against you.

Investments: Be diversified, know your risk tolerance, know your objectives.

Taxes: You want to maximize your returns and minimize your taxes.

Retirement: Maximize your contributions with your employer. You want to be investing and saving 20% of your income toward retirement (long term) and 10% (liquid) for other investment opportunities.

Estate: Make certain you conserve your estate and you have plans for your final wishes.

Mortgage: Selecting the right mortgage for your situation can save you tens to hundreds of thousands of dollars over the life of your mortgage.

Social security: Make certain you know the facts and plan accordingly.

Just a reminder: here is your road map to financial freedom and independence. Only a careful financial plan can make a difference between a *secure future* and an *uncertain future*. What path will you take? You owe it to yourself and your family. I know you can do it. *Just believe it and you will achieve it!*

Here are the steps for you to take to achieve financial freedom and independence. This is the *action* you need to take now.

1. Sit down and determine what your goals are and what you wish to achieve within a time frame.

2. Take a notebook (tablet) and record all of your expenses and record where you spend your money for the next 30 days. After the 30-day period, analyze where you spent your money and eliminate wasteful spending immediately.

3. Create a budget by utilizing the form in this book and adhere to the budget. Use the envelope or can system to allocate your money to tithe, pay yourself first, pay your bills, and so forth.

4. Work to eliminate all consumer debt and work toward paying off your mortgage early to become totally debt-free.

5. Complete the sample balance sheet in the book to get a bird's-eye view of your financial picture. Determine what your net worth is and strive to increase it annually.

6. After you have eliminated consumer debt except for your home, you must create an emergency fund. First tithe your 10 percent to the Lord and then save at least 10 percent of your income until you have amassed 6–12 months of income for emergencies.

7. Check all of your insurance to make certain you have the proper coverage. Adjust your coverage according to your needs.

8. Start to invest for short-term, long-term, retirement, and educational goals.

9. Make certain you have a will, guardianship, trusts, and so forth

10. Review your financial plan and budget annually and adjust accordingly to consummate your goals.

Whatever you need to do to become *debt-free* you must do. You must *change* the way you *think* and *handle money*. Remember it's all *attitude!*

Some or all of the following items may have to be *eliminated* to help you become debt-free.

- Cable bill
- Internet bill
- Vacations
- Entertainment
- Eating out
- Buying clothing
- Gym membership
- Coffee from places like Dunkin donuts or Starbucks.
- Smoking—cigars, cigarettes; besides this will improve your health by eliminating smoking.
- Phone bill—just have one phone line or just a cell phone not both.

If you have more than one car, sell the other cars and pay down your debt. You will also save money on gas, repairs, and insurance. An automobile is an asset that depreciates.

The only thing I am against is skimping on is eating. If you sacrifice eating healthy food another problem could emerge: health problems. Buy quality food and cook it at home. If you become sick from eating unhealthy food then what? If you can't work due to health conditions, you will never get out of debt. Do not sacrifice your health!

Try to be conscientious about your water, gas, and electric use. Do not use excessively. You could be throwing money away that can be used to pay down your debt. Get a second job to help pay down your debt. It won't be forever. Some of you may even have a special skill or hobby that you can turn into extra income to reduce your debt. *Do you get the picture?*

** I strongly suggest after training yourself in accounting for your money and paying off consumer debt, work on applying additional funds toward your mortgage principle. After your mortgage is paid off you will be totally debt-free. Won't is be a blessing to wake up *debt-free*. It sure will be! Just put your mind to it, move forward and get it done.

This is the allocation you must strive for to consummate the mission.

- Tithe   10%
- Save   Save 10% emergency fund, keep it liquid, after your emergency fund is established, keep saving 10% for investment opportunities.
- Invest 20% for retirement
- What you should be able to live on 60%

One last thought: the reason to heed to this book is that money in itself does not bring you happiness, but it gives you options. For example, it gives you options to retire, buy a second home, go on missions trips, give to charities, take care of a family member, help a fellow man, and invest in the kingdom of heaven. Make certain you give yourself options!

People Don't Plan to Fail. They Fail to Plan.

Action Plan

_____

_____

_____

_____

_____

_____

_____

_____

_____

_____

_____

_____

_____

_____

_____

_____

_____

_____

_____

_____

_____

_____

_____

_____

_____

_____

_____

_____

_____

_____

_____

_____

_____

Action Plan

Appendix 1—Stories

Story 1

*B*ack in September 2011, I was introduced to Bob. Bob needed help with his finances. He was totally upside down with his finances. His finances were in such chaos that he did not know where his money was going. I completed a needs analysis and discovered that Bob needed to be put on a budget immediately. He needed to begin to take charge and have complete control over his money. His money was controlling him. The way he was spending money was out of control. Bob has a multi-six-figure income but has nothing to show for it.

I introduced Bob to the envelope system and asked his wife Linda to get involved in the process. She was more than willing to accede and get her family's finances in order. I am still working with Bob and Linda and working on establishing a budget and emergency fund with them. I am showing them how to think differently and evaluate wants versus needs.

There is one aspect of their situation that I want to share with you. Linda does not work. Bob is the sole breadwinner and in case of his premature death, Linda would have no income. Unfortunately they have no savings and no investments. Bob showed me that he has a $1,000,000, 10-year term insurance policy with an annual premium of $2,040.00. I congratulated him for wanting to protect his wife in case of his premature death. I asked Bob how he determined that he needed $1,000,000 to leave his wife. His answer was reasonable. Then I proceeded to ask him why term insurance. He told me that it was inexpensive, and he wanted to invest the difference. Bob never invested the difference. That's why he has no savings or investments. He and Linda have no retirement money. Nothing!

I noticed that Bob had taken out the insurance when he was 55 and at age 65 the insurance will end. My question to Bob and Linda was, will Bob renew the policy at age 65? Their immediate reply was yes. I asked at the tune of $37,030.00 for year 11 and then $42,170.00 in year 12. Their reply was, what are you talking about? I showed them how Bob's insurance will increase each and every year after year 10. Simultaneous they said, we can't afford that. I said, I know. When Bob is 75 years old, this insurance that originally cost $2,040.00 annually will now cost him $119,120.00 annually. Unfortunately, Bob will lose his insurance at age 65 because of the cost. The problem is, Bob still needs the insurance, but he will not be able to afford it. Whoever recommended term insurance to Bob made a terrible mistake and left Linda out in the cold. See, Bob still needs the $1,000,000 of insurance because of all the outstanding bills that he has amassed and other obligations. Bob is in trouble because of bad advice.

Story 2

Ms. M. has been my client since 1984. I have been coaching her in financial matters and preparing her tax returns over that period of time. Over the years she has thanked me for my financial advice and my concern about her well-being This is what she told me. I want to thank you for hclping mc to buy thc co-op that I presently live in. Your financial coaching and keeping me accountable has afforded me the ability to own two pieces of property in the United States. In May of 2012, I was able to retire from the Board of Education with a very comfortable retirement. You helped me to design my 403b and showed me how I could maximize my annual contributions. You also showed me what mutual funds to invest in. I do recall when you first established a budget for me and I was reluctant to use your envelope system. I am glad that I listened to your advice, because today I am free to do what I want, when I want. Ms. M. was able to retire at age 56, with no debt and a nice portfolio of investments to live on. I appreciate Ms. M. giving me the credit, but I have to thank my Lord and Savior for giving me the knowledge and a willing heart and thirst to help people with their finances.

Story 3

Ms. L. first became my client in 1998. I first started out just preparing her income tax returns. Periodically she would call me and ask my advice on investing, savings, and mortgages. One day she called me and asked me how she could pay less in federal and state taxes. I advised her to increase her contributions into her retirement program at work. She appreciated the reduction in income taxes she had to pay. In October of 2012, Ms. L. finally allowed me to sit with her to establish a financial road map for her and her husband and to get on a budget. I met with her about three times to get her financial house in order. In August 2012, she called me and stated that I had uncovered areas of her spending that she never thought about before. She started to look at her budget differently.

Ms. L. did not like spending her money frivolously on items that she really did not need. There were other items that troubled her as well. She said I know that it took some time for the light bulb to go off. But after you established a budget for me, I started to think about things I never thought of before.

Ms. L. decided to cut back on certain expenses and eliminate others. She is now looking to downsize and move into a smaller home where her expenses will be less and other expenses to maintain her home will be eliminated in her new home. Ms. L. realized this through the use of a budget. Today she adheres to her budget like white on rice. The beautiful thing is that she sees progress in her life and in her husband's life. She is on her way to be totally debt-free. In the first quarter of 2013 I received a call from Ms. L.; she thanked me for helping her change her life. Praise Jesus!

Story 4

I was not going to tell my own story, but my son Rocco insisted that I tell our story and the struggles that we were confronted with when we moved from New York to Tennessee. What I am about to tell you may seem unbelievable but it is true. I am not exaggerating at all. When I lived in New York I had no idea how blessed I really was. I was earning a great living that I was able to save/invest 30 percent of my income each and every year. My wife and I lived within a budget. My wife was a domestic engineer and home-schooled our three children. We never did without and our children were involved in many extracurricular activities including sports and music. Our life on Long Island in New York was great. We had no debt and we owned our home free and clear. Life was beautiful.

In 2004 we decided to move to Tennessee for our children. What I did not know was that my life, my family's life would change forever. I was now in the South, and I was considered a Yankee. Finding work was very difficult for me. People living in the South did not want a Yankee for a financial coach. Just to put this into perspective, I was called an alien and a foreigner by prospective employers. One man even went up to my wife when he found out that she was from the North and stated "we are still fighting the civil war down here." Life was definitely not the same for my family and me.

For the nine years living in Tennessee I was mostly unemployed or way underemployed.

Unfortunately, for my family and me I was more unemployed then underemployed. The reason why I am telling you this is because life is not peaches and cream, and there will be hurdles that will confront you. Will you be prepared for those obstacles? Back to the story: during those nine years, I had three children who attended college. As any parent knows, college is expensive, but so are the books. Every one of my children needed transportation to get to school. This is not New York where mass transit is all around you. Now remember my situation; I was unemployed mostly or by far underemployed. Life was far from easy in the South.

What I am about to tell you is not bragging. When it comes to finances and money, I take it very seriously. I did not know it at the time, but when my Lord and Savior was instructing me to be a financial coach in New York and was telling me to make certain my own my financial house was in order, that one day I would have to use my emergency fund to live on. Because I heeded the Lord's advice I was able to sustain my family. Without my financial house in order I would have been in the street within six months. But here is what I was able to do because of a budget, emergency fund, the right kind of life insurance, and investments. My wife and I paid for every one of our children's college expenses and bought them each a brand-new car. We also were able to fund their music and CD recordings. If is wasn't for the grace of God and the financial acumen that He gave me we would have been devastated. Once again, please I am not bragging or showing off. I want you to understand the importance of proper financial planning. It is imperative to everyone's future. I hope and pray that **you and your family** will never have to live through this. It was a very uncomfortable time in our lives.

I was able to keep us afloat because we lived within a budget and did not deviate from that budget. When my wife went shopping she would look for sales and use coupons to save money. She also bought in bulk to save money. I used our emergency fund money, investment money, and dividends from our whole life policies to live on. The way I paid for our children's education and cars was from the investing I started for each of them when they were first born. Thank God I did not have to touch money from the insurance policies I bought for each of them when they were 15 days old. There are certain investments that were earmarked for retirement for my wife and me that I locked up so we would not have immediate access to them.

This is all part of preparing for the future. I told you my story because this can happen to anyone, at any time in your life. I am no one special; I do not have a crystal ball, and I am not some Rhodes scholar. I am just the quintessential Rocco. What I am is pragmatic, disciplined, determined to go above and beyond for my family and my clients, and willing do the savings/investing and budgeting that others will not do. It's all up to you. I do not want anyone to ever be in the situation my family and I were in. But if it does happen to you, wouldn't it be nice to know you are ready to weather the storm.

Story 5

My wife and I have some dear friends who where living high on the hog when they got hit with a severe blow. The husband lost his business, and the wife was a stay-at-home mom. The income just stopped. Imagine that, no income. The sad part is they never planned for the future. No savings, no emergency fund, no investments, no retirement money, nothing, zero. The one thing they do have are many bills. They owe everyone and their mother. High credit card debt, auto loans, household bills, etc. I tried fruitlessly to sit with these dear friends, but the husband was too embarrassed to consult with me or anyone else. One thing these friends of mine learned immediately is that bills are never late and they just don't go away on their own.

Please consult a professional who can help and offer assistance to you. Do not let your pride or obstinacy stand in you way from seeking professional financial help. You owe it to yourself and your family.

Appendix 2—Some Thoughts to Ponder

Do not let foolish pride stand in your way. If you need help seek it. It's okay to seek help. I do and so should you.

Proverbs: 16:18. Pride goes before the destruction, a haughty spirit before the fall.

Proud people take a little account of their weaknesses and do not anticipate a stumbling block. They think they are above the frailties of common people. In this state of mind they are easily tripped up. Ironically, proud people seldom realize that pride is their problem, although everyone around them is well aware of it. Ask someone you trust whether self-satisfaction has blinded you to warnings signs. He or she may help you to avoid a fall.

I have to stress this: do not live beyond your means! For those of you and you know who you are, who cannot control your spending habits, take your credit cards and perform plastic surgery. Get rid of them immediately. Everyone needs someone to be accountable to with their finances. A financial coach is a good way to start: someone who is going to coach you and not sell you products and will have your best interest and that of your family at heart. It's okay to have help. If it's a financial book that can hold you accountable, that's okay to. Some people would rather talk to someone than read a book. I prefer both. I read devotional books to hold me accountable to the Lord because I do not have a Christian mentor.

Here are some things I would like to share with you that I have learned and adhere to.

*Yesterday is history; tomorrow is a mystery, so focus on today. You cannot change the past or predict the future, so concentrate on today and go forward.

*To succeed we must focus in the root, not the fruit. (Dr. Ron Jenson) root-behavior, fruit-result.

*There are three basic principles for making sound decisions: (1) Get the facts before answering; (2) Be open to new ideas; and (3) Make sure you hear both sides of the story before judging.

*People who do not pay them selves first after tithing, but pay their bills first and then try to save money from whatever is left over, always come up short. This happens because there is nothing left over. Forget that idea; it is a bad one. These people will rarely get ahead. After tithing, pay yourself first, than pay your bills. When I say to pay yourself first, I mean make certain you are contributing to a retirement program, and you are investing systemically in an investment where the money comes directly from your paycheck or checking account. If you do not do this, you will not be financially successful. If you follow and heed this advice, you will unequivocally see enormous progress and money will not be an issue.

*Attitude is everything and is essential not only to your financial health but to your everyday health in general. Attitude equals 100 percent. So have a positive attitude and let your attitude be contagious to others. Your attitude will change your life for the better in everything you participate in.

Appendix 3—Principles to Live by *Faith*

F = Freedom

A = Attitude

I = Income

T = Teachable

H = House

*I*n order to achieve financial *freedom* you have to have the right *attitude,* protect your *income* from the threats of uncertainty, make the right investments to make your *income* grow and protect it against inflation, you must be **teachable**, willing to learn and adhere to the principals of this book and keep you financial *house* in order. Once you do that, you will reach *financial freedom* and *independence.*

Faith is reliance, loyalty, complete trust in GOD or someone else.

Matthew 6:27. Who of you by worrying can add a single hour to his life?

Worry may damage your health, cause the object of your worry to consume your thoughts, disrupt your productivity, negatively affects the way you treat others, and reduces your ability to trust in God. Being concerned is different than worry. Worry immobilizes, but concern moves you to act.

Have the *faith* to trust in God and Jesus your Savior and move forward with the principals of *faith* listed above.

Appendix 4—Third-Party Information

———— ❦ ————

This was taken from Kiplinger magazine March 2013; American General ran an ad. I decided to place this ad in this book because I found it very interesting. Here it goes:

"Much has been said about universal life with term insurance. Term policies offer an excellent bargain with very reasonable premiums during the term period ... but what happens after the term? Typically the rates will be significantly higher to in order to continue the coverage, or require evidence of insurability to "requalify" with a fresh set of term rates. Either way, term rates will eventually become cost prohibitive. And what if you become uninsurable during the term period? It is for this reason that less than 2% of all term policies ever pay a death claim."

Just be careful what life insurance you are buying. As I explained in the Life Insurance chapter, term insurance has its place but there is nothing like permanent insurance. It will always be there when you really need it. When I read the article I was shocked that less than 2% of all term polices ever pay a death claim. Take it for what it's worth.

One again, Thank you for taking the time to read this book. Now put it into *action* and change your *life forever*.

In His Service,
Rocco

APPENDIX 5—IMPORTANT PAPERS AND INFORMATION

Keep these important papers in a safe deposit box or in a fireproof box.

- Bank Accounts:
  - Name and address of Bank
  - Type of Account(s)
  - Account Number(s)
- Safe-Deposit Box Location
  - Location of Keys; Note: In most states, upon death, a decedent's safety-deposit box cannot be opened unless an executor or administrator of the estate has been appointed or in the presence of a tax agent.

- Location of:
  - Birth Certificate
  - Children Birth Certificates
  - Marriage Certificate
  - Deeds and Titles
  - Mortgages and Notes
  - Credit Cards and Numbers
  - Computer Password(s)
  - Last Will and Testament
  - Military Discharge Papers
  - Income Tax Records

- o Life Insurance Policies
- o Annuities
- o Other Documents
- Name of Executor/Executrix
  - o Address of Executor/Executrix
  - o Telephone Number of Executor/Executrix

Medical Information and Insurance Policies

- Doctors:
  - o Name and Type of Doctor
  - o Address
  - o Phone Number
- Hospitalization Information
  - o Insurance Company Name
  - o Telephone Number
  - o Group Number
  - o Membership Number
- Insurance Policies
  - o Company
  - o Telephone Number
  - o Name of Insured
  - o Amount of Benefit
  - o Beneficiary
  - o Location of Policy
    - Be sure to review your beneficiary selection annually. This may eliminate possible problems for your survivors. When making a claim, insurance companies require a certified copy of the Death Certificate. It is wise to make other family members, your attorney, or close friend aware of your insurance policies to ensure that claims are properly made. Also make certain that the whereabouts of your important documents are known.

ENDORSEMENTS

More than a dozen years ago a friend recommended tax accountant Rocco Vignola, after listening to my complaints about several unsatisfactory experiences with tax preparers. After speaking with him on the phone, I felt that Mr. Vignola was well informed and committed to providing the best service to his clients. This turned out to be correct evidenced by the consistency of the high quality service I have received since then. I have especially appreciated prompt and comprehensive replies to telephone and email communications. I believe his communication style will make his upcoming book very useful to every taxpayer.

Dolores McClain, Retired Teacher
New York City Public Schools

A dedicated accountant, advisory and friend, Rocco is a true professional and a proven expert in the field of finance. For the past ten years, his personal attention and advice to my accounting needs is always effective, on point and greatly appreciated.

Lisa Chappell, Administrator
Ameriprise, New York

I appreciate Rocco's financial planning and tax preparation expertise thru the years. Under his guidance I have been able to make sound investment and prepare for my future.

Gina Marie Locoparra
Owner of Crystal Clean, New York

Rocco, you are more than a consultant, I call you my friend. You have taken the time to make sure I am updated on new tax changes and always looking out for my very best interest when preparing taxes for my brothers and me. Thank you for your help and guidance when tax season was over. You didn't disappear after April 15.

Erma Casterlow, Retired
New York Telephone Company

I happened upon Rocco Vignola as a new math teacher in one of the most difficult schools in NYC school system. Unbeknownst to me, after many years of completing my taxes I was on *The Road to Financial Freedom.* He has suggested a financial consultation, and from that day on my life has changed. That consultation prompted me to look at my financial state, my financial choices and my financial prognosis. It is because of Rocco, that I am living in peace and moreover, debt-free.

Leslie David, School Administrator
Boces, New York

Mr. Vignola has been my accountant for the past three years. He has always provided sound financial advice and handled even my most complicated tax preparations with ease. He is always available to answer any financial questions that I might have. He is friendly, personable and a pleasure to do business with.

Stephine Vanino, Human Resource Specialist
Bergman County N.J Board of Social Services

I've known Rocco for the past six years. I've found Rocco to be very knowledgeable and passionate about helping people succeed in business as well as in life. He has a passion to help people to manage their financial life and has offered me sound advice to prepare myself and my family to survive today's economy as well as a plan for my retirement. Thank you, Rocco.

Bruce Loeffler,
Owner of Enspiron Training Company,
Brentwood, Tennessee

Mr. Vignola, we are writing you to thank you for all the years of friendship and personal attention that you have shown our family. It's because of you and your wife and family life that encourages my husband and I to get on the right track to get our financial freedom and get our house in order. We just wish that we would have know you much earlier in our lives. We could have done so much. But thank God for people like you. You are making a difference in so many people lives and ours as well. May God continue to bless you and your family in all you do. You are a financial and spiritual blessing to so many families Mr. Vignola.

Blessings to you and yours,
Mr and Mrs William Robinson
Robicon Productions, Brooklyn, New York

Appendix 6—The Envelope System

I have a separate envelope for each of my expenses:

Mortgage payment or rent payment   _____
Real estate taxes   _____
Telephone—landline   _____
Telephone—cell   _____
Gas   _____
Electric   _____
Credit cards—have an envelope for
  each card   _____
Insurance—auto   _____
Insurance—life   _____
Insurance—major medical / dental   _____
Personal loans   _____
Student loans   _____
Other debts—envelope for each one _____
Food   _____
Education expense   _____
Clothing   _____
Entertainment   _____
Gasoline   _____

Tithe   _____
Savings   _____
Pocket money   _____

Investments-have an envelope
for each investment   _____

If self employed
Federal income taxes   _____
State income taxes   _____
Local income Taxes   _____
FICA Taxes   _____

TOTAL MONTHLY OUTLAY   _____

X 12

TOTAL ANNUAL OUTLAY   _____

- Envelopes are used for these items if you are self-employed. If you receive a W-2 from your employer you can discard these items.

Have an envelope for any other expense or savings item you have.

This will give you a bird's-eye picture of your outlay.

Balance Sheet:

Assets:

Cash Equivalents   _____

Checking Accounts   _____

Savings Accounts   _____

Life Insurance Cash Value   _____

Cash   _____

Miscellaneous   _____

Total: _____

Invested Assets:

Common Stock   _____

Corporate Bonds   _____

Mutual Funds   _____

Vested Pension Benefits   _____

Retirement Plans   _____

Miscellaneous Investments   _____

Rental Property   _____

Total: _____

Used Assets:

Residence   _____

Personal Property   _____

Automobile   _____

Miscellaneous   _____

Total: _____

Grand Total: _____
                                                _____

Liabilities:

Credit Cards   _____

Automobile Loan   _____

Mortgage Balance   _____

Student Loans   _____

Personal Loans   _____

Miscellaneous   _____

Total: _____   _____

Net Worth: _____
                                                _____

Formula: Assets—Liabilities = Net Worth

An individual's net worth is the amount remaining after subtracting from the sum of his assets any creditor claims against the assets. The bottom line is; it is not how many assets you own, it's how many of those assets are owned *free and clear*. That's the key; to own everything you possess *free and clear* from any debt.

As you can now realize, your objective is to own everything free and clear, to buy with cash and to *be totally debt-free.*

Your Budget

Your Total Salary _____

Spouse's Total Salary _____

Total Income _____

Monthly Expenditures:

Home Mortgage/Rent _____

Real Estates Taxes _____

Telephone/Cable _____

Gas/Utilities _____

Fuel-Oil _____

Credit Cards _____

Insurance (Auto/Home) _____

Insurance (life/Health _____

Medical Bills _____

Loans/Debts _____

Transportation _____

Food/Groceries _____

Education _____

Clothing   _____

Entertainment   _____

Gasoline   _____

Payroll Taxes   _____

Pocket Money   _____

Savings   _____

Tithe   _____

Other   _____

Other   _____

Total Expense   _____

Net Surplus/Deficit   _____
                                     _____

It is imperative to complete this budget form and adhere to it.

About the Author

*R*occo Vignola is the founder and CFO of *Human Financial Health.* Human Financial Health was formed with you, the wage earner in mind. The company has dedicated itself to helping individuals just like yourself to learn how to handle money and stay debt-free.

After graduating from Herbert H. Lehman College in the Bronx with a Bachelor of Science Degree in Accounting, he started to work for the attorney general's office as an auditor investigator. Rocco learned very quickly how to pay attention to details and never leave any stone uncovered. After several years with the attorney general's office Rocco wanted to use his accounting background and get more involved in personal finance.

In October of 1983 The Prudential gave birth to Rocco, and his life changed forever. He was hooked on helping individuals, families and businesses get control of their financial house and help them to achieve financial success with their money and live a debt-free life. His spirit, work ethic, and tenacity quickly got him recognized with The Prudential. He was awarded many accolades at The Prudential for outstanding financial service and leadership. Rocco was asked to speak at many Prudential offices, districts, associations, on how he was changing peoples financial lives for the better.

His passion for helping everyone to get their financial house in order became so contagious that the company wanted Rocco to duplicate his efforts by showing other financial advisers what to do and how to do it. So Rocco assumed a new role and started to recruit, train, and develop new advisers on how they should help all people they came into contact with to achieve *financial freedom and independence.*

Everyone who came into contact with Rocco immediately realized that he was a true servant to all and was willing to share his ideas and strategies with others. Rocco is an altruistic individual who wants to educate everyone into being financially free from the worries and woes that improper handling of money can bring. Even after all these years of serving people financially and helping so many achieve their bliss financially, Rocco is still humble and always available and willing to serve. His objective is to change the way people think and handle money.

He has been married to his lovely bride, Lucia, for over 31 years. She is a Christian writer and serves the Lord each and every day of her life. Lucia has given Rocco the three joys of his life, his three children Olivia, Rocco, and Luciano. He is a family man devoted to serving the Lord and his family.

Rocco is a native New Yorker from the Bronx. He can be reached at: website: www.humanfinancialhealth.com, email:humanfinancialhealth@gmail.com

Appendix 7—Think About This

———— ‹✣› ————

J esus told His friends stories to help them learn important lessons. Matthew 25:14–28 is one of the stories Jesus told. Once there was a very rich man who owned a large house and lots of land. He had many servants to help him take care of his property. One day he told his servants that he was leaving town on a long trip. He chose three workers to be in charge of his money. He gave the first worker five talents. That is equal to about five thousand dollars! The rich man gave the second worker two talents. That is equal to about two thousand dollars. Then the man gave the third worker one talent. That is equal to about one thousand dollars. The master left on his trip and trusted the servants to use his money in a smart way—to earn more money for him.

Soon the first servant began to find ways to put that money to work for the man. Little by little, the servant used the five talents to earn more money. Finally the money doubled into 10 talents. At the same time the servant with the two talents worked and worked to earn more money for his master. He doubled his money too. He had four talents.

The third servant was afraid that he would lose the one talent that the rich man gave him. He made the decision to hide the money so that he would not have to worry about what the rich man would say. He dug a hole in the ground and buried the money in a secret hiding place. So, the third servant did not do any work, and he did not earn any extra money for his master.

Finally, one day the rich man came back from his trip. He eagerly called the three servants into his office to see what they had earned for him. The man with the five talents said, "Here sir. You gave me five talents and I have earned five more."

"You have done a good job!" the rich man said, "You are a worker that I can trust. I

will put you in charge of much more because I know that I can trust you."

Next, the worker with the two talents said, "Here are the two talents you gave me. I have also earned two more talents."

"You have done a good job!" the rich man said, "You are a worker that I can trust. I will put you in charge of much more because I know that I can trust you."

Finally the third worker spoke up. He carefully brought the rich man the one talent that was given to him. He said, "I was afraid this one talent might get lost or stolen. Then you would have been angry with me. So I decided to dig a hole and hide the talent to keep it safe."

"What!" the rich man angrily said. "You could have at least put the money in the bank to earn interest instead of doing nothing!"

The rich man took the money and gave it to the first worker because he did what the master asked.

We are responsible to use well what God has given us. We need to be good stewards of God's money. The issue in the above scripture is not how much we have, but how well we use what we have. You have the God-given ability to earn money. What you do with that money is what will separate you from being in debt and a slave to that debt, or being emancipated from debt and earn the financial stability of being in control of your money. Remember only two things earn money: people and money. Anytime you feel yourself going astray, just read the scripture.

References:

All Scripture verses are taken from the New
International Version (NIV)—1984

Kiplinger Magazine—March 2013

Life Underwriter Council (Individual Insurance)—1984

Look for the upcoming book release by Lucia G. Vignola on the hot topic, "Mold: The Silent Killer" The Nightmare and Growing Epidemic of Mold, Mold Exposure and what steps to take to save yourself when it happens to you.

Look for the upcoming book release by Lucia G. Vignola "When God Amputates You" When the Rubber of your Faith Meets the Road of your Life!

CPSIA information can be obtained at www.ICGtesting.com
Printed in the USA
LVOW05s1041220514

386785LV00003B/8/P